Before I Forget

Essays of an Old Seaman

By Gordon Thompson

Copyright © 2022 by Gordon Thompson.

All rights reserved. No part of this publication may be reproduced, distributed, or transmitted in any form or by any means, including photocopying, recording, or other electronic or mechanical methods, without the prior written permission of the author, except in the case of brief quotations embodied in critical reviews and certain other noncommercial uses permitted by copyright law.

Cover photograph by — Gordon Thompson
Back cover photograph by — Gordon Thompson
Cover design by — Dorothy Loges

Printed in the United States of America.

Library of Congress Control Number: 2022934843

ISBN	Paperback	978-1-68536-431-1
	eBook	978-1-68536-432-8

Westwood Books Publishing LLC
Atlanta Financial Center
3343 Peachtree Rd NE Ste 145-725
Atlanta, GA 30326

www.westwoodbookspublishing.com

ACKNOWLEDGMENT

I wish to thank Mary Lee Jackson for her valuable assistance in editing and preparing this book, my wife Betty for her encouragement, and countless others who have made my experiences possible.

Scientific information presented herein was learned from college courses, from reading and from many sources – most of which I cannot remember.

The Internet also played a large part in bringing up-to-date developments and additions to the literature.

Personal names have been omitted for privacy reasons, except for references to my own family.

Index

The Great Depression 1
Our Parent's World 4
How Time Goes By 6
Going Home 8
My Uncle Travis 10
That Wondrous Ark 12
Santa Sophia 14
A Flashback in Time 16
The Lepers of Calcutta 17
Dry Bones 19
The Burning Ghats of Calcutta 20
Grounded 22
Noah's Flood A Drop in the Bucket 24
The Razor Strap 26
Noah's Cubit 27
Earth's Amazing Skin 30
Dodging the Ice 31
The Buddha 33
Hearing the Echo 35
The Mysterious Coriolis 36
The Polar Front 38
Air, One of God's Miracles 39
The Sed Rate 40
Where Ships Go 41
The Dead Zone 43
The Navigator 44
Ampolletta 46
The Churning Winds 49
Shaking Off the Salt 51
Rhythms of the Sea 54
Tools of the Trade 56
The Nature of Snow 58
The Unwashed 60
The Face of Hunger 61

Sven, The Lonely Swede	63
Observing the Pelican	66
Footprints From the Arctic	68
Thermodynamic Miracle	70
Jerusalem	72
Trip to Damascus	76
The Engineering Curse	78
A Strange Confrontation	80
The Last Reunion	81
Reflections on Being Poor	82
Remembering the Weather	83
Riding the Bumble-Bee	85
Edible Obnoxious Weeds	87
Premium Pay	88
Christmas Shoes	90
The Money Counter	91
The 'Possum Eaters	93
The Truck Ride	94
The Swimming Hole	96
A Rabbit Hunt	98
Oklahoma Weather	100
A Friendly Banker	101
Chili Supper	102
Tricks of the Mind	104
A Tender Farewell	106
A Camel Ride	107
Magic Fireplace	109
The Lighthouse	110
Can Mother Rabbits Cry?	112
On Fishing	113
Where Do They Go?	114
My Court Martial	115
Epilogue	119
References	119

FOREWORD

This book was written foremost for the education and entertainment of my grandchildren and their children by exposing them to historical and scientific ideas and facts not taught in schools.

My personal experiences are secondary to the underlying themes presented, and serve only to emphasize the marvelous harmony and purpose of God's Wonderful World.

Gordon Thompson

The Great Depression

I am among the dwindling few who can still remember the Dust Bowl and the Great Depression. A primary contributing factor for this historic disaster, in addition to antiquated banking laws, was the enactment of the "Homestead Act" after World War I. With the stroke of a pen, a hundred million acres of the High Plains west of the 100th Meridian were opened for settlement. The virgin prairie, at elevations from 2500 to 6000 feet above sea level, was buffalo country with waist-high grass as far as the eye could see. Farmers rushed in to bust up the deep sod and plant crops. It didn't seem to matter that rainfall averaged less than 20 inches per year. If it would grow tall grass, it would grow wheat and cotton.

For a time the High Plains were America's breadbasket. Then, in 1931 the rains stopped. Deep plowing had killed the native grasses leaving the ground exposed to the wind. Dust clouds spread eastward to the Coast, and as far north as New York. "Black Blizzards", they were called, which shut out the sun and plunged the world into darkness. As in Biblical times, there was no "Balm in Gilead". There was no place to hide.

The drought and sandstorms would last for several years. By the second and third years, five hundred thousand people in Texas, Oklahoma, Kansas, Nebraska and western Colorado were forced to abandon their homes. A third of those immigrants were professional people from failed businesses, and 43% were farmers.

Oklahoma was one of the states hardest hit. Dad's crops burned up in the fields. Our pasture stopped growing, and our livestock was beginning to starve. Our milk cows stopped giving milk, and our diet relied heavily on cornbread and beans. After two years of drought we were barely hanging on.

The Federal Government, under FDR, passed the Soil Conservation Act in 1933, aimed at changing the farming practices on the High Plains. Congress also set up the Federal Surplus Relief

Corp for the purpose of buying up all the starving cattle that could not be sold on the open market. The SRC heavily impacted our household.

I can remember the day the government agent came to our house. He judged all five of our starving cows to be unfit for human consumption. He offered $14 per head to have them killed and buried. We were shocked at the thought. Those cows had furnished us milk and butter for several years – how could we kill them? But time had run out for us. There was no grass in our pasture, and no money to buy feed. We had arrived at a point without options, so Dad reluctantly agreed. We were allowed to keep one cow, and process one of the slaughtered ones for food. The County furnished a canning machine to help us save the meat. It was a temporary delay in the starvation we faced.

The following year, 1934, was another year of little rain, and another crop failure. Dad wanted to give up and head west to California, as half a million others had already done. But Mother didn't want to go. She was an optimist, and believed the rains would come.

At that critical point in our lives another option opened up to us. Western Oklahoma had reported a fair cotton crop that Fall. If nothing else, we were workers, and picking cotton was something we were good at. So we loaded up Dad's Model T Ford truck and, like the Joads in "The Grapes of Wrath", we swallowed our pride and headed west. We picked tons of cotton that fall, one bole at a time. When the season ended, we had enough money to carry us through the winter and buy feed for our remaining livestock.

By the end of 1935, 19 states had been declared a Dust Bowl. The Civilian Conservation Corp was formed to make work for millions of the unemployed. They built rock buildings, roads and parks all across the country. They also planted 20 million trees from Canada to Abilene, as a windbreak. New farming methods had been implemented to prevent soil erosion, and by 1936 the Great Plains, west of the 100th Meridian was fundamentally changed. Its economy was back to grass and cattle, and the dust storms were reduced by 65%. And that was the year that the rains came back. The out-migration did not return, but a new method of farming the Plains was made possible by the opening up of the Ogallala Aquifer in 1940, for irrigation. The Aquifer is a glacial reservoir underneath Nebraska, the Oklahoma panhandle, the Texas panhandle, parts of New Mexico, Colorado and South Dakota.

We have nearly forgotten the 33 sandstorms that rolled across Oklahoma in 1933-34, but we will never forget the threat of starvation that our family and livestock faced during those difficult times.

Our Parent's World

My father was born in 1890, and my mother was born in 1896. It was a challenging time to be born. Life expectancy was 47 years. Thirty percent of all deaths were children under the age of five. Pneumonia, diarrhea, diphtheria, and influenza were the major killers. Appendicitis and TB were often fatal, as were some infections, and Polio was untreatable.

It was in the aftermath of the Civil War that they came, with their parents, to settle in the untamed West. The Era of Gunfighters, Outlaws, and Bandits was coming to a close. Solitary psychopaths like Bill Langley, Clay Alison, John Wesley Hardin, and William Bonny (a.k.a. Billy The Kid) had all been killed. Wild Bill Hickock, the deadliest Marshall of the frontier, was killed when Dad was two years old.

The Indian Wars were winding down. Custer, along with his 226 soldiers had been killed by Sitting Bull, Crazy Horse, and their allies, at the Little Bighorn in 1876. The Indian Treaties of 1840-1870 had reduced Indian lands by 174 million acres, opening up new lands for settlement. Geronimo surrendered at Fort Sill, Oklahoma in 1886 marking the end of his threats to New Mexico and Arizona, which encouraged more settlers to move west.

Then, in 1889, lands not assigned, in the Treaty of 1839, to the Choctaws, Cherokees, Chickasaws, Creeks and Seminoles for their relocation from east of the Mississippi, was offered to settlers through a series of horse races. At the same time, assigned lands could be purchased from Indian tribes with the approval of the Indian Agency – thus making practically the entire territory available for a price. My grandfather may have obtained his homestead that way.

Life on the frontier was not easy. Everyone was a farmer, rancher, gambler, or a banker (sometimes called Bank Robber). Legal jurisdiction was county-by-county, with only a single U.S. Marshall responsible for the entire territory. A bandit needed only to outrun a posse across the county line to be free. The territory was a favorite hangout for outlaws.

It was a tough life, but pride in our nation had begun to stir a spirit of unity. In an inspiring historic event, Frederic Auguste Bartholdi had fashioned a colossal statue and called it The Statue of Liberty, and donated it to the United States in 1883. That same year, Emma Lazarus wrote these immortal words:

> Give me your tired, your poor,
> Your huddled masses yearning to breathe free,
> The wretched refuse of your teeming shores,
> Send these, the homeless, tempest tossed to me,
> I lift my lamp beside the golden door.

The era of people wanting to come here has never ended. But many of our people seem to have forgotten our proud heritage and the sacrifice of the millions who have died to preserve it.

I salute my parents' generation for their legacy that helped me find a better life. It is a heritage I hope to pass on to my descendants and others.

How Time Goes By

When Grandfather Sims brought his family west from Tennessee to the Oklahoma Territory in 1901, Mother was only five years old. He cleared some land and built a house on Four Mile Road south of Wynnewood. It was a "Box" house, as was common in those days, erected on wood blocks set on top of the ground. The walls consisted of 1' x 12' boards placed side by side with no stud framing to support them. Batten strips covered the cracks between the boards on the outside, but there was no insulation on the inside. Ceilings were omitted altogether leaving every room open from the floor to the shingles on the roof. A pot-bellied stove heated the living room, but the bedrooms were the same temperature as the outside. At best, it was only slightly better than living in a barn.

When we moved in to take care of Grandmother Sims, the house was already 30 years old. Wind whistled through the walls, up the floors and under the shingles. Mother added wallpaper, which helped a little, but in the winter snow somctimes covered our beds when we woke up in the morning. It was a grueling test of endurance to survive. Mother doctored us with kerosene, Vicks Vapor Rub, and castor oil for everything that needed doctoring. Like most children of that day, we caught all childhood diseases that came along. Seven of Mother's nine children survived to become adults, which might be considered a miracle in itself.

In her devotion to cleanliness, Mother insisted that we take a bath once a week whether we needed it or not – even in the wintertime. She would place a #2 washtub near the potbellied stove, fill it half full of hot water, then add shavings of lye soap which she made herself. Each kid, from the smallest to the oldest was required to bathe – all in the same water. My eldest sister, Jenny was always last and complained that she came out dirtier than when she went in. She got little sympathy from the rest of us. Rinsing was not an option, so we smelled of lye soap from one week to the next. In school I was called the "soap" kid, which put me in the category on par with skunk scent for popularity.

Compared to her sister's and her brother's kids who lived on our road, mother believed (and she was seldom wrong) that we were the prettiest, the smartest, and the most wonderful kids in the world. I don't remember hearing anyone else saying that, but it still could have been true.

Basically, we lived off the land. We raised our hogs, chickens, and most of what we ate. Potatoes, turnips and canned foods were stored in a root cellar over the winter. We had milk, butter, eggs, cornbread and molasses, which made up a well-balanced diet. When our pork ran out, rabbits and squirrels took its place. We were seldom hungry.

As a cook, Mother was from the Pioneer "cremation" school. Most everything was fried in hog lard until it was black, especially the pork. Cholesterol had not been discovered yet, and no one in his right mind would use that tasteless hydrogenated vegetable stuff called shortening. By today's standards, Mother's cooking would be considered a lethal weapon. But when she celebrated her 100th birthday she made it known that she was totally unimpressed with modern dietary theories. To her, turnip greens fried in hog lard was soul food good enough for anybody.

Today, the old homestead is an unfamiliar place. The old house has been replaced, but the land seems so much poorer, drier and more grown up with weeds than when I was a kid. There is another change more profound than that of the land - it is the haunting loneliness that envelops the countryside. The folks that lived nearby are all gone. Uncles, aunts and a bunch of cousins who once played there have all passed on, or moved away. The laughter that once echoed up and down Four Mile Road has been replaced with an eerie silence - interrupted only by the wind. That silence is a vivid reminder that God gives us what seems to be a long time to grow up, but so little time to grow old.

Going Home

If you weren't born on Four Mile Road you wouldn't want to live there. This is Southern Oklahoma where hot winds blow in the summertime, and the old days of my parents don't seem relevant anymore. This is the country where we once rode horses on dates, and where the woodlands and prairies were our playground.

Here was the last refuge for the Sims, Thompson and Clure families, all transplants from Tennessee, who moved westward to escape the moonshine culture, and to find a better place to raise their children. As settlers here in Indian Country, they put down roots that lasted three generations. My generation was the first to leave.

Picture Four Mile Road, where the old Homestead is. To get there drive south out Main Street in Wynnewood, Oklahoma on old Highway 77, past the Oil Refinery and the Block Factory on Big Sandy. Continue on past the Scruggs place and the once productive Eskridge Farm, where the orchards were. The road bends southward and skirts the Washita River Valley that was once filled with people and houses, but is now a vast hayfield. A little further south you will suddenly see the Old Joy Schoolhouse, standing empty and forlorn as if in mourning for all those kids who once filled its halls and classrooms. Today there are no children there. Houses we once knew have disappeared as if they were never there, and the land returned to Nature.

One more mile southward brings you to Four Mile Road, a single lane ribbon of gravel that turns eastward at the curve of the highway, and disappears into the emptiness of the countryside. It is now a wilderness road, submerged in weeds and grass that covers everything but the tracks. This lonely road was once lined with the houses of families named Wilson, McGee, Ketner, Clure, Stultz, Sims and Thompson. When Grandfather Sims settled there at the turn of the century he carved out a homestead along a little creek valley, and made a place to raise his family. Mother was only four years old then.

The place looks so empty now. I remember the old log barn with the sagging roof, the little orchard of plum and pear trees, and the blackberry patch that Grandmother planted. All have vanished without a trace. A few pecan trees still remain, but everything is grass and weeds.

Four Mile Road, where I grew up, is not home anymore, if home is where your loved ones are. The emotional bonds have shifted to the graveyard in Wynnewood, where Mother, Dad, three brothers, a sister and a host of friends and relatives lie buried. This is where I go when I go home, for the memories.

Before I Forget

My Uncle Travis

When Dad was ten years old, in 1901, his father died and his mother remarried a tall gun-fighter type of a man who turned out to be cruel to Dad, his two brothers and his sister. Half-brother Travis was born in 1906 and he too felt the whip when he turned old enough to work. When Dad turned fourteen, he ran away from home – never to return. The other brothers and Travis followed Dad's lead when they reached their teens. None went past the third grade in school.

Travis turned out to be quite gifted at making people laugh with his twangy voice and funny grin. He could make up a funny story on a moment's notice, and used this talent to get free meals everywhere he went. He soon learned that he didn't have to work – just make people laugh, and he was welcome anywhere. Free moonshine usually went with the meals, and Travis became an alcoholic before he reached twenty years old.

I first met Travis when I was eight or nine. Dad had banished him from our house because he "drank", and Mother called him a "good-for-nothing Hobo" (which he was). But he showed up one day, all neat and clean, and sober, and was in instant hit with us kids. We sat for hours enthralled with his funny stories – which he never seemed to run out of. He stayed a week, about the limit to his sobriety, with Dad fussing because our work wasn't getting done. Travis went with us to the fields, but he never touched a hoe or a shovel. His job, he said, was to keep us happy. That he did with a massive talent concealed behind a façade of ignorance and cloaked in the garb of a Hobo.

Travis never married, although everyone seemed to like him. He was as gentle as a puppy. If he had an ambition no one ever knew. His wealth was never more than what he had in his pockets, and the clothes on his back. He never owned a car or a place to lay his head. His bedroll was an old raincoat in which he would bed down wherever night found him.

For more than fifty years he came and went like a phantom in the night – touching our lives as no one else could. He continued to make us laugh, even when we could see the sadness in his eyes. The last time I saw him walk away (always at sundown), my heart ached for him. I knew that he had no place to go – but he "had to go". Stooped and gray, and slow of pace, he was a victim of countless miles and fruitless years. He had played his cards with a losing hand, and was left with no chips to cash in.

He suffered a stroke, and spent his last years in a County Care Facility in California. All of his worldly possessions were stored in a little box at the foot of his bed. We are not sure just how, or when, he died. Perhaps he died of a broken heart - abandoned by the countless people who were cheered by his stories. He was buried in a Potters Field with no one there to mourn his passing. My Dad was dead, as was his other brothers, and Mother was unable to go.

If we measure success by the money we make or the things we accumulate Travis was a total failure. But if we measure success by the laughter we have brought to the lives of others, Travis was a giant among men. The world could use more like him.

Before I Forget

That Wondrous Ark

Some scholars dismiss Noah's Ark as a biblical fantasy with no relevance to today's world. However, since 250 BC, when Archimedes discovered why objects float, man labored to find that magic shape for a ship's hull that would break through the hydraulic speed barrier that kicks in at about 10 knots for all submerged hulls. Although the Ark was not built for speed, understanding the sheer genius of its design awaited the coming of the Renaissance Period and great minds of men like Galileo, Newton, Pitot and Bernoulli who laid the foundation for modern hydraulic theory.

By 1850, other great minds like Euler, Rankin, Reynolds and Chezy had perfected the theories of how water flows in pipes and defined that unique relationship between fluid flow, pipe size and resistance as the "Hydraulic Radius" of a circular tube. This discovery made possible the piping of water and sewage in Medieval Europe, which, in time, would end the scourge of Typhoid, which had ravaged Europe for 300 years.

By 1870 Dorcy, Cutter and Manning had defined a similar "Hydraulic Radius" for an open trench. They discovered that least resistance and maximum flow of water in a trench is realized when the depth of the stream is one-half its width. Similarly, a ship's hull submerged to half its width presents the least wetted surface and the least frictional drag for its total weight.

Let me refer you now to the dimensions of Noah's Ark given in the seventh chapter of Geneses. It was 50 cubits (75 feet) wide, 30 cubits (45 feet) high and 300 cubits (450 feet) long. With only a few cubits left above the water line, the submerged depth was approximately half its width giving a Hydraulic Radius similar to that defined by Dorcy, Cutter and Manning. It is evident, therefore, that the ratio of dimensions of the Ark was almost identical to those of modern merchant ships. For example, the Liberty Ships of World War II were about 50 feet wide, submerged to 25 feet when loaded, and were 450 feet long. That design didn't just happen that way. It was the most efficient high-volume low-speed hull modern science could devise.

So, that wondrous Ark, constructed millennia before the world discovered why rocks don't float, was built to near exact specifications currently applied by the builders of modern ships. And perhaps even more amazing, it was three times larger than any other wooden ship ever built – a staggering feat requiring human knowledge that did not exist in Noah's day. One cannot dismiss Noah's Ark as a biblical fantasy without also dismissing God as a fantasy.

Santa Sophia

On a cargo stop at Istanbul, my immediate focus was to visit the world's most magnificent Byzantine Church. Set on a hill inside the ancient walls, its awesome beauty can be seen for miles. It represents the apex of Byzantine Art. Architecturally, it is of "Central Design", with a massive dome set on pendentives, and is more refined that San Vitale, or Sant'Apollinare in Ravenna. The unique design consists of an arrangement of arches and half-domes merging in increasing size and volume until they unite in the all-embracing dome which covers everything.

At the dedication, in 537 AD, Paulus Silentiarius, Court Poet for Justinian, wrote these words:

"About the center of the church, by the eastern and western half-circles, stand four mighty piers of stone, and from them spring great arches like the bow of Iris, four in all, and they rise slowly in the air, each separates from the other to which it was first joined and the spaces between them are filled with wondrous skill, for curved walls touch the arches on either side and spread over until they unite above them.

The base of the dome is strongly fixed upon the great arches, while above, the dome covers the church like the radiant heavens. How can one describe the fields of marble gathered on the pavement, and the lofty walls of the church? Fresh green from Carystus, and many-colored Phrygian stone of rose and white, or deep red and silver: porphyry powdered with bright spots; emerald green from Sparta, and Iassian marble with weaving veins of blood-red and white: streaked red stone from Lydia, and crocus colored marble from the hills of the Moors, and Celtic stone, like milk poured out on glittering black:

The precious onyx, like as if gold were shinning through it, and the fresh green from the land of Atarax, in mingled contrast of shinning surfaces.

Gordon Thompson

Thin pieces of marble are fitted together with inter-twinning tendrils bearing fruit and flowers, with here and there a bird sitting on the twigs. The Capitals are covered with the barbed points of graceful acanthus, all gilt, but the vaulting is covered over with many little squared of gold, from which the rays stream down and strike the eyes so that man can scarcely bear to look.

Characters and episodes move in hieratic succession from scenes relating to the life of the Virgin and of Christ, through the figures of Angels, Saints and Prophets on the walls, to the four Cherubim in the pendentives, and finally to the Pantocrator, the Ruler of the Universe, in the crown of the dome, with the inscription 'Know and behold that I Am'. Thus the movement of lines and volumes is paralleled by a literary movement of ever-increasing sanctity and awe culminating in the symbol of the heart and mystery of the Christian Faith."

Santa Sophia, along with the Gothic Cathedrals of Notre Dame, Rheims, Cologne, and Chartres stand as the few remaining Great Wonders of the World.

A Flashback in Time

After the war, the world's trade routes were flooded with about everything that would float. From old coal-fired buckets which trailed a cloud of black smoke from one continent to another, to sailing vessels of all types. In the coastal waters of Europe and Asia, we were on constant watch for small craft near large ports. Such sightings were routine, but I was not prepared for what crossed our path in India.

We were slowly making our way up the Ganges to Calcutta, when our Lookout alerted us to something special off the starboard side. We stared in disbelief. There, right out of medieval history, was an oar-powered Galley inching its way upstream. It was powered by ten oars on each side, with two men on each oar working to the rhythmic beat of the Boatswain, at about fifteen strokes per minute. Such a cargo vessel was largely abandoned by the time of Columbus in favor of the mast and sails, and could not exist except in a country of abject poverty, like India.

I was moved by the sight, and of being witness to a form of slavery believed to have vanished centuries ago.

But even today, Galleys such as that may still be working the Ganges.

Gordon Thompson

The Lepers of Calcutta

In preparation for our trip to India we were given vaccinations for all the common diseases to be encountered there – except Leprosy. There was no Leprosy vaccine then, and still none today, more than half a century later, because the Mycobacterium leprae cannot be replicated in a Petri dish.

Leprosy, perhaps the most feared of all the ancient diseases, is a bacterial infection that attacks the skin, flesh, nerves and outer extremities of the body. It forms nodules, ulcers, and white scales and, over time, eats away infected flesh. Although not easily spread, infected people have been separated into enclaves since 1898. India, with its indigenous poverty was hard hit and maintained more than a thousand Leper Colonies, (and still do) one of which is located on the outskirts of Calcutta. Even the United States maintained a Leper Colony on Molokai until after the War. One hundred twenty-two countries still considered Leprosy a public health problem until 1985, when more effective treatment became available.

The Colony in Calcutta was a walled compound with an open gate. Lepers were forbidden to mingle with the public, but medical people and visitors had access to the gate. When I arrived to have a look, some people were already there, giving food and medicines to the inmates. I was shocked and appalled to see their condition. The Lepers were forbidden to hide their infections, and most wore only a loincloth for clothing. They appeared to have no bedding or eating utensils, and ate with their hands to avoid any contact with others. They were

Before I Forget

poorly cared for, as evidenced by the smothering odor that filled the compound. Their helplessness helped me to understand the cries for mercy of Lepers in biblical times, when it was a disease that no man could help and only God could cure.

Leprosy was the mechanism by which God chose to reveal Himself to Naaman through Elijah (2 Kings), and was used by Jesus to reveal His healing power in Matt: 8. And like the sins of the world, Leprosy seems to be always with us no matter how good our medicines are.

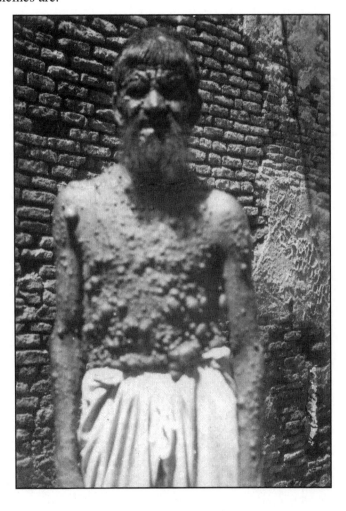

Gordon Thompson

Dry Bones

Right after the war we were delivering wheat to a starving Calcutta in the oppressive heat of August. I was fascinated by the Sikhs, a hereditary Hindu social class which believes in one God, prohibits idolatry, and does not bury their dead immediately after death. The word was that they deposit their dead on the roof of the Temple until the bones are picked clean. They then collect the bones for burial in their ancestral tradition. The Temple roof is a sacred place where no Infidel is permitted to look. But I was no ordinary Infidel and didn't take their traditions seriously. I "just had to see" what was up there.

Access to the roof was via a spiral staircase in a Minaret located on one corner of the building. At midday, when most everyone was sleeping, I sneaked into the minaret, thinking that no one saw me and headed up the spiral stairs. As I neared the top, I heard a loud commotion below me in the stairwell. I knew I was in trouble. There was no place to run. As the angry mob approached, fists shaking, I tossed them my camera and put on my "Tourist Stupidity" act, a tactic that had served me well in other forbidden places. They were not amused.

They stomped my camera and drug me down the stairs into the courtyard, where they promptly tossed me over the fence. No resistance was offered on my part.

I got no pictures. But I walked away with a memory that few Baptist Infidels have shared.

Before I Forget

The Burning Ghats of Calcutta

As I walked along one of Calcutta's crowded streets, I heard a disturbance coming in my direction. Suddenly, the crowd parted and four joggers, bearing a stretcher on their shoulders, came into view.

They were carrying the body of an adult that was wrapped in white cloth. To find out what was going on, I picked up their pace and fell in behind where others were following along.

In a mile, or so, the joggers turned toward the Ganges River and entered a walled compound which stretched for half a mile along the riverbank. Several fires were burning and a stench filled the air. It suddenly dawned on me that this was Calcutta's Burning Ghats, a self-service, open-air crematorium for a Religious Sect that believes that once a person dies the body must be immediately burned to prevent evil spirits from entering in.

The joggers proceeded directly to a pre-arranged pyre of wood, placed the body on top, and set fires in several places around the pyre. Within minutes there was a roaring blaze which forced

people to move away. To my surprise, there was no funeral service, no singing, no sermon and no crying. Family members stood around, some talking, some eating food they had brought, and some making themselves comfortable for a process which could take many hours. The atmosphere was unemotional, even detached from the anguish and sorrow I had expected. Several fires were burning, each with its group of family members keeping silent vigil for their dead.

When the stench became unbearable, I retreated outside the wall and headed back to town. Other runners were coming as Calcutta's teaming millions meet their fate one by one.

I felt a deep sadness for these people, whom I didn't know, because they had probably never heard of Jesus, and the Resurrection and Judgement that is sure to come.

Grounded

During Summer Break at the University of Oklahoma, it was my custom to work as a crewmember on a ship sailing out of Baltimore to earn money for my tuition for the following year. As a member of the National Maritime Union, I could apply for a job on any ship, which needed a crewmember with my qualifications. I had papers for Able Seaman and Quartermaster, whose job it was to steer the ship into and out of ports, up rivers and through canals. It was a job I was good at and one I enjoyed. Some older ships and new Liberty ships were built like a bathtub, and were especially hard to handle, particularly when nearly empty. But none of that mattered when you needed a job, so I signed on as Quartermaster.

It was a Liberty ship bound for ports in Europe, which would let me get back in time for the Fall Semester. I turned my card in and was on my way the next day. We would deliver cargo to Germany, France and Holland; and also take return cargo for Boston, Philadelphia and Baltimore. This would require passing through the Boston Canal, going up and down the Delaware River and through the Chesapeake Canal to Baltimore. I didn't give it a second thought.

The trip went well. The Boston Canal had no current when we passed through and the Delaware River had maneuvering room; but the Chesapeake Canal, which connects the Delaware River to Chesapeake Bay, presented a special problem – the tide was flowing at 2 knots in our direction of travel. The Liberty ship, now nearly empty, sat on to of the water like a cork with only a third of its rudder in the water. Steering was sluggish even without the current.

Normally we would have waited for the tide to change, but time is money for the ship owners so we entered the canal knowing that maneuvering could be a problem when speed was limited to 5 knots. The canal, only 400 feet wide, provided no room for error since only half the width could be used if opposing traffic were encountered. Controlling the 10,000-ton ship turned out to be work. I was constantly over steering to compensate for the several seconds in lag time from the rudder. But things went well until we met another ship on the first curve. Both ships slowed for the passing, which diminished what little control I had. By the time the other ship had passed we were drifting out of control toward the south bank with no chance to recover. We ploughed into the mud, and lodged there unable to move.

Bedlam broke loose with many angry words and choice phrases all aimed in my direction. For a moment I feared for my life. Explanations were useless. It was pilot error, pure and simple, to enter the canal with downstream current in the first place, and to cut power at any time in the second place. But in the heat of the moment it was all my fault. A Coast Guard Inquiry would be called to resolve the matter.

A tugboat was dispatched from Baltimore to pull us free and a new pilot came aboard to take us the rest of the way to Baltimore. My part in the inquiry was simple. All I had to say was that we lost steerage due to inadequate speed. Propeller speed recorders confirmed that power was cut off for two minutes during the turn, which placed the blame on the pilot, where it belonged.

It was a bad experience that I was happy to have behind me as I headed back to school.

Noah's Flood
A Drop in the Bucket

Perhaps those who dismiss Noah's Flood as an impossible fairy tail should refer to the Biblical accounts, which indicate that conditions were different then.

We read in Genesis that the life span of the generations from Adam to Noah, excluding Enoch, who walked with God when he was 365 years old, averaged 862 years. During that period, before the flood, many believe that a dense cloud mass covered the Earth shutting out the sun. The first mention of the sun coming up, or going down is made in Genesis 15 - after the flood.

Scientists have estimated that the amount of water carried in a cubic mile of Cumulus clouds at 70,000 tons. No one knows how thick the clouds were in Noah's day, but to shut out the sun for all those years they would have had to be exceedingly thick. Even by today's standards, 86 million tons of water evaporates from the oceans and the Earth's surface every day. If that amount of moisture were to accumulate for a year, or hundreds of years, and then fall in just 40 days, a flood of historic proportions would occur.

Modern day examples confirm how fast rain can fall:
In July 1911 the town of Baguio, in the Philippines, reported that two feet of water fell on two consecutive days – the equivalent of 80 feet in 40 days.

In November of that same year, a weather station in Panama reported 45 inches of rainfall in one hour – the equivalent of 90 feet in one day.

In northern India the city of Cherrapunji reported a rainfall of 905 inches in one year – nearly 75 feet of water over everything.

Other examples abound.
Noah's Flood happened as punishment for Man's sins and was just a drop in God's bucket, from which other judgements are sure to come.

Before I Forget

The Razor Strap

When we kids needed an attitude adjustment Mother's favorite weapon was a switch made from a peach tree limb. When heavier artillery was required Dad would bring out his razor strap – made of heavy leather and capable of doing serious damage to one's backside. I remember one such occasion.

My cousin Calvin received a new BB gun for his 8th birthday. (Calvin and I were the same age.) We sprayed the countryside with pellets, shooting at anything that moved, and much that didn't – including writing our names with pellets on the wall of our Smoke House.

One day, perhaps out of boredom, we noticed Dad's prize bull grazing peacefully with our cows. His tail was toward us and his private parts dangled temptingly as a target for our expert marksmanship. Without considering the consequences, I took careful aim and unloaded a pellet to his most tender spot. The bull, normally a gentle pet, let out a bellow that could be heard half a mile away. He bucked and pawed the ground in instant rage. We raced for cover just as Dad emerged from the barn to see what was going on. He guessed immediately what we had done.

As he applied the strap unmercifully to my backside, I could hear Mother laughing hysterically in the kitchen. But it wasn't all that much fun for me.

Gordon Thompson

Noah's Cubit

When Noah built the Ark, the standard of measurement was the cubit. That cubit, subsequently used by the Sumerians and Egyptians, was defined as the length of the forearm from the point of the elbow to the end of the middle finger. It depended entirely upon the size of the person doing the measuring. Other forms of measurement in use at the time included the "digit" (the width of one finger), and the "palm" (the width across an open hand at the base of the fingers). All of these methods were quite imprecise and no two items were built exactly the same size.

When the Greeks became a world power, they came up with the Olympic Cubit and called it a "foot". The Olympic Foot was defined as the width of 12 thumbnails as a way of improving accuracy. The Olympic Foot was adopted by the Romans, and later passed on to the British where it became merged with the Anglo-Saxon measures being developed independently. Thus, the Anglo-Saxon "fathom", which was the distance across two outstretched arms, became equal to four "cubits", or six "Olympic feet". Confusion reigned.

During the time of the Norman Kings (800-1200 AD), "half a fathom" was found to be a more convenient measure, and was defined as the distance from the center of the chest to the tip of the outstretched arm. Then came Henry the First, who decided to simplify the system. He issued a decree stating that "the half fathom" would henceforth be defined as the distance from the point of the nose to the end of the thumb when the arm was fully outstretched. Not content with this momentous improvement, he further decreed that the half-fathom would henceforth be called a "yard". This abominably inaccurate "yard" is still being used today. (Mother used to buy dry goods that way.)

The search for a workable standard of measurement rocked on for another 400 years. Then, in 1558 Queen Elizabeth I, who wanted all her ships to be the same size, made another historic decree. She ordered her "Exchequer" to fashion a brass rod one yard

Before I Forget

long, mark it into three equal segments and each segment would be called a "foot". So, for the first time in the history of the world there now existed a standard length to which all other measuring devices could be calibrated. Queen Elizabeth's "Imperial Yard" became the universal standard, which in 1856 was adopted by the Office of Weights and Measures as the standard of the United States.

Of course, not everyone was happy with the "Imperial Yard". The French promptly declared the English System "stupid" and proceeded to come up with a system of their own. The French Academy of Sciences calculated the diameter and circumference of the Earth and divided its meridian quadrant into 10 million equal parts and called that measurement a "Meter". In 1888, the meter became the foundation for what we now know as the Metric System. By 1927, the Metric System was fully defined and became a second set of standards for the world to use.

But trouble loomed. The brass yardstick fashioned by Queen Elizabeth expanded and shrunk with temperature changes, and was not accurate enough to be used as a true standard. Many other metals were tried until finally a platinum-iridium bar, held at the melting temperature of ice, was adopted by the International Bureau of Weights and Measures as the standard "yard" and "meter". The temperature reference was changed from 32 degrees F to 62 degrees F in 1929, and then to 68 degrees F in 1932, where it remains today. Finally, the world had a standard of measurement accurate to one part per million for all to use.

But the question was asked, "What if those precious bars were destroyed by fire or earthquake?" Could they ever be duplicated? The answer sprang from Professor A. A. Michelson, who in the 1930's developed a method for measuring the wavelength of light - a mechanism called an "Interferometer". Using pure red light emitted by a cadmium vapor lamp, he determined that there were 1,553,164.13 wavelengths to a standard meter. At long last an indestructible definition of a meter became the heritage of mankind.

Then in 1940 at the University of California, a Dr. Alvarez discovered that by bombarding gold with neutrons from a cyclotron he could transform gold into "pure mercury 198", which, when excited by radio waves, emitted a single frequency light many times stronger than cadmium red. This increased the accuracy of measurement from one part in 1 million, to one part in 10 million. That is where we are today.

Noah's cubit was millions of times less accurate than what we have today, but it didn't matter. What mattered was his vision and his faith which, in comparison to our own, cannot be measured.

Earth's Amazing Skin

Like an onion, the sky has many skins of global layers, invisible but real. Numb spots of poorer circulation occur randomly, such as the Sahara High, and the Indian Dome, both areas of tropical stagnation. Above these "weather areas" the temperature drops dramatically to −70 degrees F seven miles up. This marks the bottom of the cold clear cloudless layer called the Stratosphere. The Stratosphere extends up to about 30 miles where the temperature abruptly rises from the absorption of the Sun's rays. This "warm" layer, called the Ozone Layer, extends up to about 37 miles. Above that marks the beginning of the Ionosphere that stretches out to infinity, or as far as air molecules go.

Approximately 15 miles into the Ionosphere (50 miles up) comes the frigid layer where radio waves begin to bounce back to Earth. All space above this level has little air and is called the deep Ionosphere, the habitat of meteors and auroras. This raw outer skin of the Earth's atmosphere is our frontline insulation against the scorching blast of the Sun, and the never-ending hail of charged particles and objects from outer space.

This atmospheric onionskin makes life on Earth possible and is another one of God's miracles.

Gordon Thompson

Dodging the Ice

On our way to Europe we were warned to be on the lookout for a line of icebergs drifting south about 200 miles off Newfoundland. I wondered where they were coming from.

Because the Bering Strait is narrow and shallow (less than 50 meters deep), the inflow of salt water into the Arctic Ocean is small. Fresh water flows in from surrounding continents via the MacKenzie River in Canada and the Ob and Yenisey rivers in Siberia. A current develops with the aid of inflow north of Norway that causes an outflow near Greenland. This forms the cold Labrador Current that transports the icebergs southward.

Thousands of icebergs break off from Greenland's hundreds of glaciers each year. Most collect in Baffin Bay until they melt, but some drift around Davis Point and into the Labrador Current, which carries them into the North Atlantic. Only three or four hundred reach the shipping lanes to Europe, and of those only a few are large enough to be detected by radar. But even the small ones, weighing only a few hundred tons, can be a hazard to shipping.

The iceberg danger zone extends from 40 degrees North to 60 degrees North, a latitude from Baltimore to the tip of Greenland; and from 30 degrees West to 50 degrees West covering the mid Atlantic. Few have been sighted outside this zone. The Titanic struck an iceberg 100 feet high by 400 feet long at 41 degrees North and 50 degrees West, just barely inside the danger zone. Today such a large chunk of ice would have been detected by radar.

When our radar picked up the first iceberg it seemed so small and insignificant. As we moved closer others came into view, all in a line as if tied together. Not all were white. Some had dark stripes caused by successive deposits of summer pollen and moss separated by winter layers of packed snow. Some had deep blue areas from old hard-packed deposits turned solid. Their shapes were jagged and irregular. They had survived the Gulf Stream but were

Before I Forget

melting rapidly. Even so they would pose a threat to shipping for weeks to come.

Other sources of icebergs in the world are less threatening. Those in the Gulf of Alaska are held close to the shoreline by the Japanese current and pose no threat to shipping. Those that form in Antarctica are of a different category. They are tabular (flat topped) and huge. In February of 2009 a chunk measuring 3000 square miles in size broke away from the Mertz Glacier and is now floating just off the continental shelf. It is fortunate that there are no currents to take that iceberg northward where it could play havoc with shipping lanes, and even affect the climate of some coastlines.

This, I believe, is all part of God's Plan.

Gordon Thompson

The Buddha

While touring the many places of worship in Calcutta, I came upon a huge statue of a Buddha surrounded by people. Perhaps eight feet tall, the statue depicted a seated ascetic big-bellied giant wearing only a loin clothe. It stood inside a small open shelter large enough to protect it from the rain, but still accessible for people to come close for their ritual chants. It appeared to be made of concrete. There was no place to sit, nor any indication that this was a church, as we know it.

Buddhism doctrines are complicated. Each person must work out his own attainment of a Nirvana transformational experience. That experience has nothing to do with the "Hereafter", but everything to do with the "Here and Now". It is strictly on a human level, aimed at obtaining true happiness on Earth.

Meditation is at the heart of the Buddhist way of life. It leads believers to obtain a higher level of consciousness whereby they learn to identify negative thoughts as delusional, and to replace them with peaceful and positive thoughts, which makes possible a "virtuous mind". In theory, as the mind becomes more positive and virtuous, one's actions become more constructive and life becomes more satisfying and beneficial to others. Although, just how that happens is not clear.

Those who follow the teachings of Buddha are expected to move step-by-step on a path to lasting happiness, the reality of which is to rid one's self of all earthly desires and responsibilities. If total Nirvana is achieved a Buddhist could sit on a street corner and starve to death if no one brought him food, all the time feeling no obligation to work for his necessities. Of Buddha's 376 million followers, Calcutta seemed to be overflowing with them begging alms. In their exalted state they claim to be filled with universal love, compassion and spiritual power, which they are supposed to share with all mankind.

They do, however, make offerings when bowing to a Buddha statue. With hands held with palms together and placed over the heart, or on the forehead, they may offer flowers, fruit, incense or water. Each represents an aspect of Buddhist teachings. Money offering are not included because it represents greed, selfishness and the embodiment of worldly things, which all Buddhist renounce. It is strange, indeed, that Buddhism has acquired so many followers considering that it was founded by a man who made no pretense of divinity.

The founder Siddhartha Gautama was born in 563 BC in northeastern India and died in 483 BC. He is recognized by adherents as an "awakened" teacher who shared his insights to help earthly beings end their sufferings, achieve Nirvana and escape the cycle of suffering and rebirth. His place of birth seemed to have only two classes of people – masters and servants. His father Suddhodana Gautama was an elected chieftain and a member of an Oligarchy. He wanted his son to become a king, but at age 29, despite his father's wishes, Siddhartha left the palace to learn of the sufferings of ordinary people. His experience led him to abandon royal life and take up a spiritual quest embracing extreme asceticism. He practiced prolong fasting and endured severe pain until, finally, at the age of 35 Siddhartha completed his spiritual quest to become "The Enlightened One" – The Buddha. Followers soon flocked around him, and a new cult was born.

Many people still think that Buddhism is a religion, but its ideology does not advocate the practice of worshipping God, or gods, in any physical form.

Gordon Thompson

Hearing the Echo

Echoes have been a source of fascination ever since man learned to stand on the rim of a canyon and scream into the abyss to hear his words come back. That was simple echo. But other echoes have plagued societies since Time began. The words we speak may come back to haunt us as quickly as they are spoken. Secondhand echoes of that type may bear a scant resemblance to the original words.

Modern Science has given us the radar echo and radio waves, which bounce off the Ionosphere. As a by product of warfare, Nature has given us the "compound" echo of naval gunfire, which is seldom mentioned and poorly understood.

My exposure came when our ship was challenged for recognition as we ran the coast of New Guinea. An U.S. warship, barely visible over the horizon tried to raise us by Morris Code while our deck officer was busy. When we didn't answer, a shot was fired across our bow. The silent flash of the gun was followed by a period of waiting. Perhaps 20 seconds before the projectile splashed into the water a few hundred yards in front of us, we heard the muffled sound of the muzzle blast coming to us through the water. About half a minute after impact we heard the same muzzle blast coming for us through the air. In between those blasts we heard the projectile's approach – in reverse. The decrescendo of its delayed approach gave the illusion that its past was catching up to the present.

Something similar may happen when I listen to a sermon. There is a delayed recognition as my mind catches up. Sometimes I hear nothing, or the echo of other sermons bouncing around the recesses of my mind. Some sermons keep coming back, like a Spiritual Echo, until I understand.

The Mysterious Coriolis

Every ship captain and aircraft pilot must learn this important rule: keep to the right of the storms. The outer winds of hurricanes and tornadoes rotate counter-clockwise in the Northern Hemisphere. The cause is the rotation of the Earth that creates a gyroscopic force known as the coriolis. That is why an east wind spells trouble, it being a part of a storm from the west, and why the right side of a north moving hurricane is the dangerous side of forward spin. It explains why an airplane flying east is lighter than the same plane flying west, and why rockets are launched eastward ahead of the turning Earth. It is the secret of the gyroscopic compass - the ever-present centrifugal component of the net gravity.

This mysterious force is at work everywhere causing everything from spinning tops to bath tub drainage to turn one way more easily than the other. It is why the Yukon River cuts faster into the right bank than the left bank; why one-way railroads have to replace more rails on the right side than on the left side; and, perhaps, why horse racing tracts and automobile racing tracts always run counterclockwise. It is believed to be the reason why Northern Timber Wolves move in a left-handed circle around their territory. Pirouetting ballerinas, the spin of boomerangs, cowboy lassos, circling seagulls, and roulette wheels seem to follow this unwritten rule: turning left is easier than turning right. (One exception is the migrating Pelican, which sometimes circle to the right into a leftward spiraling updraft for more lift.) My dad's old horse-powered hay bailer was designed for the horse to circle to the left; and in the modern world, windmills and air turbines are designed to spin counterclockwise. Most northern nations drive on the right side of the road, and aircraft spiral counterclockwise in the landing pattern at every airport in the world.

Some of the effects of the coriolis are subconscious. Mother stirred her pot of beans to the left; I brush my teeth with a counterclockwise motion and couldn't reverse it if I tried. It is as if the human brain has adapted to the coriolis and it's controlling effects to the extent that it has become part of our instincts.

The Earth is forever turning "out from under" whatever is upon it and what strange things result from that are not strange at all. They are all part of God's Plan.

The Polar Front

We are all familiar with the dynamics of flowing winds, of doldrums and the horse latitudes; but we may take for granted one of the great meteorological discoveries of the Twentieth Century – the Polar Front.

Discovered in the early 1900's by a genius named Bjerknes, who described the Polar Front as a super front containing zones of both warm and cold air masses interacting in alternate fashion to form weather patterns around the world. It is the zone where warm tropical air flowing north meets the cool polar air flowing south. It is where low-pressure storms roll counter-clockwise between clockwise turning high-pressure masses, like ball bearings in a wheel. It is the crossroads of maximum turbulence in the sky.

In the Southern Hemisphere where west winds can blow unobstructed around the world between the Andes and Antarctica, the front confines itself largely to uninhabited lands, at latitudes between 50 and 60 degrees South. But in the Northern Hemisphere, with its jagged Rocky Mountains, Greenland's Ice Cap, the Norwegian Fiords, and the towering Himalayas, it is a different story. In this region, the Polar Front doesn't go just through the Bering Sea, the Hudson Bay, and on around the sub-arctic world, but splashes over the whole Temperate Zone from Mexico to Alaska, and from Arabia to Norway. Although semi-tropical areas such as Florida, Egypt and Indonesia may escape the worst of the storms, the United States, Canada, Northern Europe, Siberia, China and Japan feel the full force of huge churning air masses that may average only 3000 miles apart, at 50 degrees North Latitude.

These huge polar fronts move somewhat like the Sun, marching northward in the summer and southward in the winter. Fluid dynamics tells us that any surface between moving fluids will be turbulent – like that between the ocean and the air above. It is the intricate dynamics of these huge churning air masses that bring moisture to the Northern Hemisphere, where most of the world's people live. It is, without a doubt, all part of God's Plan.

Gordon Thompson

Air, One of God's Miracles

Evangelista Torricelli, Galileo's pupil, demonstrated in 1643 that air has weight and substance. Because of its weight gravity holds the airy sky to the Earth with such force that few molecules can escape. If Earth's gravity were any less it would lose it's atmosphere and become as lifeless as the moon.

Modern Science teaches us that air is a mixture of gases and microscopic dust. That dust turns out to be one of the most important molecules in the sky. It serves as nuclei for condensation. Without dust the sky would have few clouds and little rain. Dust has cleaning properties. Mohammed taught his followers to bathe in sandstorms. Even the purest air in nature contains some microscopic dust.

Air also contains viruses and protozoa that float in suspension. Shaped like strings, beads and popcorn they are the smallest and most elusive forms of life. As passengers on the wind, they move around the earth bringing epidemics to diverse locations. Only the Polar Regions escape their wrath. Humidity is their fuel. When dry they encase themselves in sheaths and remain dormant until moisture sets them free perhaps years or hundreds of years in the future. The influenza epidemic of 1918 came "out of nowhere" and killed millions of people.

But the most important element in the air is the concentration of oxygen that sustains life. God chose the numbers – 23% by weight and 21 % by volume. Oxygen is the most abundant element on the Earth's surface comprising 89% of water, 49% of rocks which make up the Earth's crust, and is a component in most compounds and in all living things. Oxygen sets the Earth apart from all other celestial bodies as a place for life to flourish. Its concentration remains essentially constant. When mixed with nitrogen in volume ratios of 21% to 78% it makes up the air we breathe.

It is another one of God's Miracles.

The Sed Rate

In physics class I remember studying the sedimentation rate of various objects in salt water. It was fascinating to learn that a grain of coarse sand might fall a foot through salt water in about a second; whereas, a particle of fine clay might take months to sink the same distance, or an estimated 15,000 years to sink to the bottom of our deepest oceans. Sed rate, we found, is a matter of weight in relation to resistance.

This came to mind when I began riding ships. I wondered what happened to bodies buried at sea. Old sailors say, without scientific proof, that weighted corpses sink more and more slowly as they settle deeper into the ocean until they eventually stabilize and remain suspended at some intermediate depth forever. Something similar happens to sinking shells of tiny coccoliths, spent plankton and other crustaceous sea creatures. Some of the larger ones reach the ooze-covered sinkholes of the deep to form a creamy colorful paste of limy disintegration. But the deepest oceans have no ooze because the particles dissolve before reaching the bottom.

As the sea has its sed rate so does the ocean of the sky. The "Glow Stratum" emitted by Krakatoa in 1883, for example, traveled many times around the Earth completing one circuit in 13 days. The ash cloud rose to twenty miles then began to settle at a rate of about 50 feet per day. After five months most of the larger particles had settled out. The microscopic bits floated on for years or never reached the Earth at all. Oklahoma sandstorms, made of courser particles, tend to settle out much faster.

Even the sed rate of mountains has been studied by scientists. Some mountains are getting shorter for the same reason people get shorter with age. Our bodies compress, our muscles weaken, we stoop and bend under the pull of gravity until the earth swallows us up.

My sed rate seems to be quickening with each passing year.

Gordon Thompson

Where Ships Go

People who ride ships travel through many passages. Harbors, lakes and rivers are common; but a few places stand out as being special. The Inside Passage to Alaska ranks near the top of the list. It zigzags through 400 miles of blind inlets with no exit in sight. Closed in by mountains on all sides it emphasizes the distortion of distance over water that is so fascinating. Such a close-up view of the mountains makes the Inside Passage a favorite vacation trip for thousands of tourists each year. Unfortunately, many tour ships run outside the Passage to save time.

Canals that connect one ocean to another are also high on the list. Suez, with its endless miles of sand dunes reaching out to the Hejaz Mountains on the east, connects the Mediterranean to the Red Sea. Straight as an arrow, this barren ditch provides a shortcut around Africa.

The Panama Canal is another engineering masterpiece. It cuts through lakes and mountains to connect the Atlantic to the Pacific. Locks lift ships up and over the Isthmus to accommodate the different elevations of the two oceans. It saves nearly ten thousand miles that would be required to sail around Cape Horn.

Canals date back to Biblical times. Darius built a canal to connect the Tigris to the Euphrates, and canal builders have been busy ever since. In the middle centuries canals were built all over Europe. In France, Italy and England canals of all sizes were constructed where water was available. The Bridgewater Canal in England is a special case. It crosses over the River Irwell on a bridge on its way to Manchester carrying coal barges to the industries there.

In more recent times canal building has revolutionized commerce worldwide. The Iron Gate, on the Danube is a good example. The Iron Gate is a narrow cut that separates the Carpathian Mountains, on the north, from the Balkan Mountains on the south, forming a boundary between Romania and Serbia. Until a few years ago, the Danube dropped 130 feet through the gorge in only 60 miles, forming rapids that severely limited boat traffic. A high dam was constructed downstream to make river traffic possible for ocean-going ships. Other dams control the water depth for river traffic all the way to Regensburg, Germany – 1770 miles upstream. At Regensburg, the headwaters of the Danube, a canal was built over the central mountains of Germany to connect the Danube to the Main and the Rhine, which flow into the North Sea. That canal is called the Main-Rhine-Danube Canal, and rises to 1330 feet above sea level. The entire system contains 66 locks, with all the water for the upper locks being pumped up from below because there are no rivers up there. The canal has transformed commerce in central Europe.

The U.S. also has canals. The Boston Canal cuts through Cape Cod and saves many miles for ships moving south. One of my favorites is the Delaware-Chesapeake Canal that connect the Delaware River to the Chesapeake Bay, forming a shortcut to Baltimore for ships returning from Europe. But one of the most unlikely canals ever built is right here at home – it is the McClellan-Kerr Canal that connects Tulsa to the ocean via the Arkansas and the Mississippi rivers. I've heard it said that if Senator Kerr had lived, the canal would have extended to Oklahoma City and perhaps all the way to Denver (just a rumor, I'm sure).

Ships have always been one of the cheapest ways to move cargo, and wherever they really need to go someone will build a canal to take them there.

Gordon Thompson

The Dead Zone

As we stood on the shores of the Black Sea at Constanta, Romania I was struck by the absence of fishing boats and pleasure craft on the beautiful waters. A question to our guide obtained the shocking answer.

The Black Sea is 160,000 square miles of captive water that has no outlet or overflow. The Bosporus allows water from the Adriatic to flow into the Black, which serves to replace some of the evaporation not covered by fresh waters from the Danube and other streams. Over eons, salt has accumulated to saturation levels such that no plant or animal life exists below 30 meters. Without nutrients the vast depths of the Black Sea has become a lifeless black hole shutting out even the sunlight that is needed for plant growth.

Some fish live in the top 30 meters but mostly near the mouth of the Danube and other fresh water streams. The Black and the Caspian together form 300,000 square miles of aquatic dead zone where even the sea birds have trouble existing.

It boggles the mind that the face of death could be so beautiful.

The Navigator

I was fascinated by the tales of my childhood Indian friend about how the Indians found their way. The Cherokees, Pawnees and the Osage found nature's compass everywhere:

> Moss grows on the north side of trees
> The tips of evergreens bend eastward
> The woodpecker digs his den on the east side of trees
> Compass goldenrod tips bend northward away from the sun
> Amber seeping from the spruce is clear on the south side, but gray on the north
> Migrating geese, flying at night, announce their southward flight

The Indians used what nature gave them to move freely across their feeding range.

Noah was perhaps the first navigator of record. In the midst of the flood he sent out land-seeking birds – first the raven, then the doves. It was the birds that told him that land was east by south.

The South Sea Islanders also learned from birds. Like the Arabs, the Phoenicians and the Vikings, the islanders kept frigate birds, which seldom rest on water, to seek out the nearest land. But the far-ranging fulmars, petrels, shearwaters, skuas, jeagers and the Albatrosses keep a peaceful tongue at sea, and lead nowhere when followed.

The Arabs were the first to use stars for navigation. They plotted the rising and setting points of fifteen stars, and added true north and south to form the thirty-two points of the compass still used today. But it was the winds and the seas that told direction as much as the stars.

The South Sea Islanders were masters at reading winds and

seas. They recognized the differences between the ripple, the wave and the swell. Ripples change with each puff of breeze; waves run before winds generated by pressure lows, and are unpredictable; but the swells, generated by the unceasing prevailing westerlies, roll across the Pacific from continent to continent unaltered by local disturbances. The wonderful stability of the swell gave the navigator a reliable compass wherever he happened to be. When swells wrap around an island obstruction they create eddies that radiate outward from the trailing edge of the landmass and point directly to the island. At night, fluorescent organisms in tropical waters light up the eddies like a beacon to safety. The Marshall Islanders plotted maps that covered much of the southwest Pacific.

Ancient mariners could get only latitude from stars. Pytheas, the greatest navigator of the ancients, visited Iceland, Greenland, Ellesmere Island and Thule. His remarkable voyage, recorded in his book "The Ocean", was largely ignored by historians of the times.

The Renaissance brought a new level of exploration.

Bartholomew Diaz cleared the Cape of Good Hope in 1487. Vasco da Gama sailed on to India in 1497.

Columbus, a devout Catholic, who learned the ropes the hard way, listened to no one when planning his voyages in 1492. He ignored the calculations of Eratosthenes and Ptolemy, who had estimated the circumference of the Earth at 24,000 miles nearly 1500 years earlier. He figured that China was 2700 miles west of Cape St. Vincent – 1100 miles short of reality. To measure speed (longitude), he chose not to use the waterwheel and the tally pot perfected by the Romans 500 years before his time.. He carried no land-seeking birds. Perhaps strangest of all, he carried no astronomer and missed the eclipses of 1494 and 1503, which could have given him the exact longitude of his newfound lands. But what Columbus had in abundance was old-fashioned courage, dead-reckoning skills and bountiful cooperation from The Almighty.

Ampolletta

An ampolleta is sitting on the mantle of our fireplace. It is a byproduct of the Renaissance when the minds of men stepped back from an inward focus on the soul to look outward to the vastness of the world to seek what wonders God had made. The immediate object of man's gaze was the vast unknown ocean around him. The challenge was how to find his way out there and back again – of going where no man had ever gone before. The secret of success resided in knowing the time and speed of travel. But there were no clocks back then.

Since Adam lifted up his eyes in the Garden of Eden to observe the midday sun, and called to Eve, "Eve, My Love, where is lunch?" and Eve replied "Adam, My Sweet, you can get your own lunch", man has used the sun to fix the time of day. In the Post Pleistocene Era of the Talgai and Sandia men, Stonehenge was erected on the plains of England as man's first sundial. Predating the pyramids of Cheops and Snefru, and the sixteen Inca Towers in Cuzco, Stonehenge was a sophisticated predictor of the Equinoxes and Solstices of the Northern Hemisphere. It measures the Polar Point, the months the days and the hour of the sun. Subsequently, the sundial became part of civilized societies long before Abraham set out from Ur.

Old Testament Hebrews had the sundial. "Isaiah the Prophet cried unto the Lord, and He brought the shadow ten degrees backward, by which it had gone down in the dial of Ahaz." 2 Kings: 20:11.

With it's center post, called a gnomon, oriented to the North Star, the sundial was the timepiece for land-based civilization well into the 18th century.

But sundials require a stable base and were useless on the rolling decks of ships. Another method of keeping time had to be found if ships were to venture into the unknown. To fill this need the glassmakers of Venice developed the sandglass calibrated to one-half hour, and the ampolleta was born.

Accurate to a few seconds per hour, the ampolleta framed the discipline and religious ritual that became the custom of the sea. Attended at all times by a young boy (ship's gromet), who's job it was to turn the sand-glass and call out the half-hour by voice, or by bell, to synchronize the crew's duties and mark the all important "time of travel" for the log. Eight ampolletas, or eight bells, made a four hour watch, which is still used on ships today.

The great voyages of Pytheas, a thousand years before Columbus, were made sailing mostly north and south using only the midday sun for a 24-hour estimate of elapsed time and longitude. But with the ampolleta explorers like Diaz, da Gama, Cabot, Frobisher, Berents, Baffin, Tasman, Cook, Columbus and the far-ranging Magellan removed the limits of man's vision of where he could safely go on the Earth. Although Columbus, and others, carried the cumbersome astrolabe for measuring the angle of the sun, it was the ampolleta that they lived or died by.

By 1700 the accuracy of the ampolleta was deemed unsatisfactory by the British Government for the rapidly growing West Indies trade. By the Act of 1714 a reward of 20,000 pounds-sterling was offered for a timepiece that could reduce the transatlantic error to one mile. Clock makers had long been busy but had yet to produce a clock that would keep accurate time at sea. Rising to the challenge was a Yorkshire carpenter named Harrison, who grasped the necessary element of keeping accurate time – a temperature compensated balance wheel and spring, and the chronometer was born. With the fourth model issued in 1761 the calculation of longitude was improved to one-tenth mile per thousand. The Harrison Chronometer became the standard timepiece of the sea until late into the 20th Century.

Even though the ampolleta became out dated it remained in service on British merchant ships until 1839, illustrating how long-standing traditions are hard to break.

Before I Forget

Captain Cook was first to use a chronometer on a long voyage. With his chronometer set at Greenwich Time, he always knew how many hours east or west he was, as measured against the local midday sun. With a reflecting sextant (already develop) he could accurately fix his latitude by the stars. Navigation had come of age.

With all the hazards and uncertainties of the sea, it is no wonder that the ancient mariners were probably the most God-fearing of men. At His mercy every hour, often drenched and half starved, the white lips of the common sailor could easily respond to the eloquent sympathy of Psalms 107:23-31:

"They that go down to the sea in ships, that do business in great waters, these see the works of the Lord, and His wonders in the deep. Oh that men would praise the Lord for His goodness, and for His wonderful Works to the children of men."

Gordon Thompson

The Churning Winds

Hurricanes are the big brothers of the Earth's churning winds that blow predominately from the west. These westerlies, moving also northward from the equator race eastward ahead of the turning Earth. In the Northern Hemisphere, these winds seem to reach maximum strength at 45 degrees north latitude but cover the entire Temperate Zone. Populated areas of the U.S., Europe and Asia are protected by multiple ranges, which moderate the velocity. But in the Southern Hemisphere, the westerlies sweep across the empty oceans at near gale force at latitudes above 50 degrees south. Magellan must have had a rough time sailing around Cape Horn going west.

The engine for these Trade Winds is the heat differential between the equator and the Poles. Airflow is constantly exchanged between the two, with vast amounts of water vapor going along for the ride. As air cools on its way northward, some of it plunges back to Earth creating rainfall and storms where low pressures exists. Air that makes it to the Pole-of-Cold flows downward and spreads out to flow south again beneath the warmer blanket of the Temperate Zone. The Pole-of-Cold is believed to lie somewhere in Siberia far from the geographic pole.

Nothing grabs a seaman's attention quicker than a tropical storm. They are awesome to behold. Such storms are born near the equator when the sea temperature reaches 82 degrees F. Long before the storm arrives the swells will slow below 8 per minute and high Cirrus clouds will cover the sun. Darker and lower clouds will soon appear followed by a black wall-cloud, perhaps two miles high, that seems to close down to the surface of the sea. Hurricane winds soon follow and the waves can reach amazing heights. By then it is too late to run.

In December 1944 we were in a convoy headed for the Philippines. Our little ship, about a third of the size of standard freighters, detoured to Morotai Island to recover fallen troops just as a hurricane passed by. The hurricane caught the convoy and Halsey's invasion fleet, which was just withdrawing to refuel. Three destroyers – the Monaghan, the Spruance and the Hull – went down. Twenty-two other ships were damaged, 146 planes were blown overboard and 790 men were lost. It was the greatest weather disaster of World War II. The Navy later reported that waves were cresting at 27 feet with wind velocities up to 110 miles per hour.

It is humbling to remember that our little ship escaped the storm only because we had stopped to retrieve the dead.

Gordon Thompson

Shaking Off the Salt

The old saying "once a seaman – always a seaman" is often true. There is a certain romance, a seductive anticipation for each new voyage that will take you to yet another country and another continent. Each voyage offers an opportunity to see and learn how other people live and, in some cases, to be thankful for the good old USA.

When I went to sea so long ago, as my contribution to the war, I had never seen a pool of water larger than a small lake and had no comprehension of what lay ahead. But ignorance can be a comfort for the innocent when grounded in romantic stories of the past. I had read about the golden age of the clipper ships, which culminated in the famous race of 1865 between the Ariel, the Serica and the Fiery Cross. Their 99-day, 16,000-mile race from Foochow, China to London framed my conception of what being a sailor would be like.

Back then I viewed the oceans as essentially vast pools of stagnant water stirred only by the winds. I had heard of the Gulf Stream, but not the other huge currants that bathe the continents in warm or cold water that determines weather patterns of rain or drought. Currents like the Labrador, the Humboldt, the West Wind Drift, the Guinea, the New Zealand, the Benguela and the Mozambique swirl the vast oceans like a mixing pump powered by temperature differences, the pull of the moon and by centrifugal forces generated by the rotation of the Earth.

Bodies of water in motion tend to flow in circles. The Gulf Stream pumps water northward along the American coast, then eastward to Europe, then southward toward the equator before turning west again. A semi-stagnant pool of water develops near the thermal center of this flow - called the Sargasso Sea, the Horse Latitudes, the Doldrums - a hazard to all sailing vessels caught unaware. Located on both sides of the Equator, the Tropics of Cancer and Capricorn form the pivot centers of the swirling oceans in both hemispheres.

How Columbus missed the Doldrums is a mystery. He sailed south of the Sargasso with the Northeast Trades going west, and north of it going east with the prevailing westerlies. This was seamanship at it's best.

Powered vessels take no note of the Sargasso doldrums except for the flotsam, which collects to impede traffic. Large masses of seaweed, algae beds and plankton collect there and draw feeders of all sizes – including whales in significant numbers. Waterspouts are churned up when the temperature builds and when the northeast trades bump against the prevailing westerlies. On one occasion we counted seven towering waterspouts in a row under clear skies, like giant trees on the surface of the sea.

The oceans are framed by a variety of shorelines. Our eastern coast and those of northern Europe and much of the Pacific Rim are low, sometimes swampy, and invisible 30 miles out. In contrast, the towering escarpment of the Brazilian Plateau, which rises directly from the sea and the coastal ranges of California, Alaska and western South America can be seen from many miles away. The shorelines of Greece, Turkey, Lebanon, Israel and the Eastern Shore of the Red Sea are arid mountains often submerged in a dusty haze with a reddish glow. The shoreline of North Africa shimmers in the heat of the Sahara giving it a character all it's own.

Rivers, too, affect the character of the sea. The Mississippi, the Nile and the Ganges color the ocean red and brown for many miles out, and red mud from the Amazon can be seen 500 miles from shore. Pale green means shallow or fresh water; whereas, deep salt water is always blue.

Where the currents go the winds follow, or vise-versa. The roaring winds of 50 degrees south latitude contribute to the mighty Humboldt, which bathes the shoreline of Peru. The North Pacific is churned by heavy winds, which follow the Japanese current northward along the Alaskan coast bringing nutrients for whales, crabs, sea lions and warmer temperatures for the rim.

Gordon Thompson

Ships have evolved a lot over the years. The Mayflower averaged 2.5 knots on her 95-day voyage to America. Two hundred years later the clipper ships could do 6 knots. Columbus and the ill-fated Bounty averaged closer to 4 knots fully rigged. Old steam-piston rust-buckets of my day could do 8 knots with a tail wind, but by the war's end things had changed. Victory ships could do 12 – 14 knots and the C-class freighters could do 18 knots fully loaded, had ample supplies of hot and cold water and were air-conditioned throughout. They were a sailor's dream.

For nearly four years ships were my home. However, being always on the move can become addictive. Lake a Hobo riding the rails, going yonder or over there becomes a substitute for doing positive things to achieve an outcome in your life. Travel becomes the mistress of the mind. At some point it no longer matters where you go as long as you are "going somewhere".

My generation of sailors witnessed the Schooner and the Tramp Steamer shake off their ancient crust of salt only to find ourselves becoming heavy-laden. It was time for me to shake off my own crust of salt while there was still time to break away. After the war a new industrial revolution was getting underway. Industry was exploding and jobs were plentiful. So when the Exporter docked in Baltimore on our return from India I said good-bye to the life of a seaman. In doing so I gave up an offer of a free education at the Merchant Marine Academy at Sheepshead Bay, New York to take my chances as an over-aged freshman at the University of Oklahoma.

Rhythms of the Sea

Part of the serenity of an ocean beach is listening to the harmonic lapping of the waves. It is the same sound one hears aboard a ship whether the ship is moving or standing still. Such a never-ending beat can be hypnotic and soothing to the nerves. It becomes an "accepted" sound and the mind takes note of any changes.

But not all ocean sounds have a pattern. Waves running through the Mediterranean Gap at Gibraltar can change daily. The measured frequency of Atlantic swells is interrupted by the choppiness of an opposing or crossing sea, and by waves bouncing off the landmass on either side. The visible change is significant too. Choppy seas look darker, similar to when a north wind blows.

The absence of wave sounds has a meaning all its own. Trailing seas that are running from behind the ship expose the ship to maximum vulnerability. The stern sits lowest in the water and can be swamped by huge waves – like those that roll down the English Channel from the North Sea. "Rollers" can ride a ship down until all decks are submerged – a situation more frightening than dangerous, as long as the ship maintains its speed.

Other sounds can be alarming on the first encounter. In the upper Bay of Bengal, where the gravitational pull of the Himalayas causes the ocean level to rise, shallow tides are magnified into a mass of whitecaps and breakers. Similarly, Mt. McKinley and the Alaskan Range contribute to the 40-foot tide that runs up Cook's Inlet to crash against the sea walls of Anchorage, Alaska like a hundred freight trains. In January, the inlet freezes over during slack tide and then breaks up with a sound like rolling thunder.

The frenzied turbulence of a tropical storm is a terrifying reminder of what the sea can do. The aftermath of such storms roll outward for thousands of miles across the globe to be encountered in unsuspected places. Late Summer and Fall reap the violence of the Hurricane Season to become the most dangerous months of the year.

Latitudes above 60 degrees, both north and south, where winds are stronger and more enduring, are where seas are roughest all year long. The Temperate Zone, which lies between these extremes, is usually a quieter and kinder place. It is in this zone that most ocean traffic occurs and it is in this zone where the gentle rocking of low swells more accurately defines the true rhythms of the sea.

Tools of the Trade

When I was growing up my 25 cent compass always pointed in the general direction of "North". Unlike ships at sea I never needed to make allowances for the Earth's magnetic fields. It was not necessary to know that the North Magnetic Pole is 1350 miles from the geographic pole, and that the two lines of zero magnetic variation wander randomly snake-like across the continents, from pole to pole.

These mysterious curves of magnetic equilibrium serve to confuse the sea-faring crowd and land-based populations who are interested in flying. Even more confusing, the isogonic lines of constant magnetism are shifting a degree or two every half century, except in four neutral locations: Lake Michigan, The Bahama Islands, Asmara by the Red Sea, and a place in the Pacific near Japan. And as all seamen know, the horizontal component of magnetic force at the equator steadily fades to a useless nothing at the poles, thereby making all compass navigation increasingly unreliable the farther from the equator one gets. It is no wonder that Peary had so much trouble finding the North Pole in 1909.

To add to the confusion of finding one's way, local micro-magnetic forces pull at the compass needle causing it to "deviate" from the normal "variations" which are calculated and mapped for navigational use. Thus, the natural magnetism of a ship's hull must be counter-balanced by a degaussing process that neutralizes its magnetic field until the compass can no longer "see" the ship. Such corrections were generally made before each trip.

To rescue ship's captains from all this confusion a gyro-compass emerged from research in the early 1900's. But it wasn't until mid World War II that a workable model could be produced in sufficient numbers to make a difference. American war ships, and some freighters, were the first to receive the mass-produced Chrysler model based on a 1911 patent by Elmer A. Sperry. This device harnesses the force of gravity using mercury tubes to a gyro-wheel so that the axis of the wheel will always seek the north-south line. The essential part of a gyrocompass consists of a rapidly rotating wheel so mounted that it has freedom of movement about three mutually perpendicular axes. The wheel fits in a mounting known as a "Gyroscope" such that it's axis of spin settles parallel with a true meridian. Gyroscopic inertia, or rigidity in space, holds the rotating wheel in a constant position as long as the ship's electrical supply is not interrupted and no external force work to disturb it.

This is all good and well except when the ship moves from one place to another. The Earth itself rolls 15 degrees every hour, and when the ship also moves additional corrections in the gyro's horizontal position are required. For example, a gyro perfectly horizontal in New York would be upside-down in Calcutta if no corrections were made. So viscous liquids and counterweights are used to keep the wheel perpendicular to the Earth's axis at all times. Of course correctional devices can be overpowered by rapid movement or abrupt changes in direction. When upset, the gyro may take several minutes to readjust.

The gyrocompass was a quantum leap over the magnetic compass in accuracy, but still left much to be desired. It provided direction but not location. The answer came with the Global Positioning System we enjoy today.

The Nature of Snow

As a kid growing up in southern Oklahoma, I was enthralled by the first snow of winter. I didn't understand it but it was beautiful. Our first snow this week reminded me of times long ago when I loved to play and romp in the first snowfall.

Unlike hail, which is born in the upper reaches of thunder clouds in summer's heat, or sleet, which are tiny frozen raindrops falling from a winter cloud through freezing air, snow has a genesis all it's own.

Snow springs straight out of the mysterious emptiness of the sky where cold winds turn molecules of water vapor into sublimated crystals without going through the liquid phase. Sublimation of water vapor can only happen when the temperature is colder than 20 degrees F below zero. The tiny crystals, starting with two atoms of hydrogen and one atom of oxygen, grow symmetrically according to the "laws of crystal lattices" to form a hexagonal symmetry which can grow in any direction. This magical process occurs because the "vapor pressure" of super-cooled water vapor is higher than that of ice at the same temperature , so the vapor drifts like a microscopic wind, down pressure gradients from water vapor to nascent ice – thus forming baby snowflakes out of an empty sky.

The tiny triangular ice seeds shoot out ice buds at angles of 60 degrees, grabbing molecules – three at a clip – as they pass by. Rapidly, the triangle becomes a prism and the prism becomes the axle, or hub, of a six-sided wheel that grows into infinite shapes having prismatic or hexagonal spool-like form. The most common shape is that of a well made wheel with a hub protruding on either side, always with one hub longer than the other. The wheel usually falls with the short hub downward creating the semblance of a tiny parachute that floats and spins in lazy decent to the ground. In sufficient numbers snowflakes insulate the Earth from radiation losses such that a snow storm may actually feel warm. As a swooping owl absorbs more sound than he creates, a heavy snowfall imposes a silence on the Earth.

Like feathers, snow, being on the average one part ice to 20 parts of air, makes excellent insulation. The igloo is one of the world's best insulated houses. Without the insulating power of deep snow, ground temperatures in our northern states would become too cold for early planting, thus shortening the growing season and crop yields.

The benefits of snow are countless. Without snow to store moisture and feed the rivers of the world famine would be an ever-present companion of mankind.

Snow is another one of God's unnumbered Miracles.

The Unwashed

I was born in an era and at a time when cleanliness was not a fetish, or even a primary objective.

We grew up playing in the dirt, swimming in polluted farm ponds and eating with unclean hands. We drank unpasteurized milk and water with 800 parts per million of dissolved solids, and thought nothing of it. We ate wild game with whatever diseases they might have had and, at times, ate spoiled food because we had no refrigeration. Our bodies built resistance to the germs, the bacteria and the microbes that populated our environment such that we were seldom sick. We lived as man was supposed to live – like wild animals without medical care.

Today we live in a disinfected world. Cleanliness has become a sacred ritual from the moment of birth. Pasteurized food and purified water have denied our children the opportunities to develop immunities that previous generations have enjoyed. One possible result could be that intestinal disease and ulcerative colitis, usually found in older people, is becoming more common in children, and tooth decay occurs at a much younger age.

No one has yet linked longevity to cleanliness but the generation born before 1900 had its share of people who lived to be 100 years old – my mother among them. Even so, one could conclude that a little soap is probably harmless, but too much soap could be hazardous to your health – at least some of my relatives think so.

Gordon Thompson

The Face of Hunger

When World War II ended hunger was widespread across Europe and Asia. The United States mounted a massive food relief effort using wheat and corn from the silos of the Midwest and from Canada. Boston and Baltimore became busy shipping points using the fastest freighters in our aging fleet. I worked the USS Exporter delivering shiploads of wheat to France, Germany and Holland where modern machinery removed the grain with huge tubes and transported it to flour mills or into storage. Our trip to Calcutta was different.

We arrived in Calcutta expecting to see modern European-style equipment ready to unload us. Instead we tied up to a barren dock with no buildings, no cranes or unloading equipment, and no trucks to carry the grain away. We were met by hundreds of people, including children, begging for food. With their arms uplifted and speaking in English, they pleaded for scraps from our table. We gladly obliged but we had very little excess food to give them. My heart ached for the children.

I noticed that many of the children had a missing arm, foot or hand. I later learned that those disfigurements were inflicted by their parents so they could better survive as beggars. Parents who were unable to feed their children disabled them and dumped them out on the streets to be at the mercy of what kindness existed in that part of the world – which wasn't much.

Policemen arrived to disperse the beggars but they simply melted into the darkness only to return at daybreak. About 200 laborers arrived to unload the wheat. They came with hand scoops, hemp sacks and sewing thread. As the sacks were filled they were placed on the dock by the ship's rigging. From there they were picked up by men on foot and carried on their backs several miles to the flourmill. Every loose grain of wheat that fell on the dock was immediately picked up and eaten by the beggars.

Before I Forget

When I was free to go ashore, I hired 15 children as guides to show me around Calcutta. The largest, a boy of 10 or 12, acted as spokesman and leader of the group. He aggressively protected me from all other beggars who wanted to tag along. When we ate or rode a trolley, he handled the money and paid the right amount. He selected safe places to eat and to shop. He also fed and dressed the little boy who had no arms. I never felt safer in a foreign place. At the end of the day I gave each one his Baksheesh (tip). Their eyes would light up in gratitude as I handed out the coins. The little boy with no arms carried his coins between his toes. When night came they huddled down together on the dock for protection and warmth.

For more than two weeks those children were my daily companions. We went everywhere together. They treated me like a king, and all they wanted in return was food and a little attention.

They were standing on the dock when we pulled away. Just babies alone in the world. I waved goodbye with deep sadness wondering what would become of them. Would they live to become adults?

Worldwide children are most often the face of hunger, and the faces of those children still linger in my mind.

Gordon Thompson

Sven,
The Lonely Swede

In May 1947 I signed on to crew the Waterville Victory, which was sailing out of Baltimore during summer break from the University of Oklahoma. It would be a short cruise to Europe earning me enough money for tuition for the next semester. It was my custom every summer. When I entered my assigned quarters the other bunk was occupied by a tall Scandinavian man with a chiseled face and short blond hair. He smoked nervously and whittled on something all the time. Over the next three weeks I would hear his incredible story of hardship and tragedy.

Sven Seleger was born in Copenhagen, Denmark in 1918. When he was little more than 12 years old the Great Depression swept across Europe destroying jobs and families like a great economic plague. Famine and starvation were widespread among the poor and the Seleger family was among the poorest of the poor. His father took what work he could find until he became too weak to work. Sven believed that his father sacrificed himself so his two children and wife could have more to eat. He died of starvation when Sven was only 12 years old.

Sven's mother, out of desperation, put Sven and his 14 year old sister, Zelta, out on the streets to beg, steal or do whatever was necessary to get money for food. She also went out to steal chickens from a nearby farm. She was soon caught and sent to prison for two years – leaving the two children to fend for themselves.

For a couple of months they survived by begging. But the city was full of beggars. One morning Zelta kissed Sven goodbye and disappeared into the city. He never saw her again.

Sven wandered aimlessly along the docks - searching always for food. One day a little dog, which had been abandoned by its owner joined him in the search. Together they survived by eating

Before I Forget

rats. The dog would catch them and Sven would cook them over an open fire. They shared an empty shipping crate as home.

One day a coal-fired steam ship came up short of crew and offered Sven a job shoveling coal. He took the job and he and his dog set out on a four-year journey together that would take them many times around the world. When the dog died Sven became desperately lonely and reckless. He married a girl in Iceland after only two dates. After a week together his ship left and he never saw her again.

Three years later, the pattern was repeated in Valparaiso, Chili. But this time he stayed two years and became the father of a baby girl. When he found himself out of work he went back to the sea to make money, and could never seem to get back home again. He wanted to go back and did after three years only to find that she had divorced him and moved away.

"So here I am", he said. "A lost soul, nearly 30 years old on this ship headed for Amsterdam where my new wife will meet me. I will leave the ship there and go with her forever, and there will be no more ships for me."

Soon we were entered the harbor at Amsterdam and headed for the grain unloading docks. Sven's wife, who lived in Rotterdam, had been told where to meet the ship. But she had not been told that we had left Baltimore a day ahead of schedule. Her window of opportunity for meeting the ship was narrower than she thought.

The unloading began immediately. Huge suction tubes were inserted into the cargo bays to transfer the loose grain directly to the flourmill. Sven took up his watch on the upper deck looking for his wife's arrival. For two days and nights he stood there, leaving only for food and nature breaks. She never came. On the third day the ship was empty and we prepared to leave. As we pushed off Sven begged the captain to let him go ashore but was refused..

We had moved out into the Harbor about two hundred yards when a lady wearing a red coat started waving to us from the dock.

Sven didn't hesitate. He jumped overboard and started swimming for shore. The alarm was sounded and floatation devices were hurled in his direction. He never looked back. We could see the tide carrying him away from his target. The Harbor Police were called and soon arrived. But in the growing darkness Sven was nowhere to be seen.

I will always believe that, with his determination, Sven made it and found happiness at last.

On his bunk he left a small suitcase containing everything he owned except a small hand-carved vase, which he had placed on my bunk perhaps as a gift for listening to his story.

That little vase is one of my prized possessions, and occupies a favored spot on our fireplace mantle.

Before I Forget

Observing the Pelican

The migration season for the Great White Pelican is drawing to a close. The fascination of seeing these huge birds effortlessly soaring in circles, ever southward, riding the wind, attests to the miracle of flight they have mastered to perfection. To watch them is to wonder why they don't fall from the sky as anything heavier than air would be expected to do. But the pelicans, and the vultures, know the secret:

Soaring in a circle allows them to spend more time climbing into the wind to a higher altitude than they spend falling on the downwind leg. By adjusting the diameter of that circle they can maintain altitude or even climb higher without flapping a wing. So round and round they go. Gravity is to the pelican as a kite string is to a kite. It holds each against being blown to leeward, thus making their airfoils more efficient.

But not all birds can soar. The narrow pointed wings of the fast flyers – like the falcon, the swallows and the swift are good examples.

The bent-wrist wings of the nighthawk, the Red Tail Hawk, the grouse, the pheasant and the quail permit power glides for short distances.

Exceptions are the long-range, high-speed soaring birds like the albatross, the petrel, the skua and the jaeger. These have extra-long narrow wings for greater lift. But, perhaps, of all birds the hawk probably contributed most toward teaching man to fly. Soaring over zones where most men live, hawks were a constant reminder that objects heavier than air can remain aloft with little effort. Their secret was discovered only a little at a time.

Lord Kelvin, renowned English scientist, once stated, "Soaring, which puzzled Solomon, puzzles me." Sir George Cayley in 1810, using the Seagull as an example, worked out the relationship between wing loading in pounds per square foot and minimum gliding speed required to stay aloft. He came up with the remarkably accurate number of 25 mph for 0.5 pounds per square foot.

French scientist Idrac, on a mission to the South Seas in the mid 1800's, noted the albatross soared at an average speed of 49 mph. These findings spurred more studies of wing shapes which resulted in two new parameters of wing design - aspect ratio and camber.

Aspect ratio is the length of a wing divided by the width. For most birds the average is 3:1. For the albatross it is 5:1. In modern aircraft it can be as much as 7:1. In general the higher the ratio, the greater the lift with the maximum being about 18:1 because of strength considerations.

Camber is the width of the wing divided by the depth of the curvature. The average camber for birds is 13:1. Slower birds can have a deeper camber of 10:1. The Wright Brothers' first glider had a camber of 22:1 and a wing loading of 2 pounds per square foot. This gave a landing speed of 35 mph.

So the pelican, the heavy bomber of the bird world, with an aspect ratio of 4:1, a camber of 11:1 and a wing loading of less than 2 pounds per square foot is one of Nature's most proficient flyers.

Footprints From the Arctic

My first assignment to crew a merchant ship was in the winter of 1943. The ship was the USS Zelinski, an Army supply vessel working out of Seattle to supply Army bases in Alaska. Our training included an Arctic Survival course in case we were forced to go ashore. My notes included the following points:

The North Pole is not a land of continuous blizzards and snow. Most of its moisture falls as rain. Most blizzards north of the coastal ranges are local, with modest snowfall. Polar temperatures can be as mild as Montana or Chicago in January between blizzards. And the Pole-of-Cold is located somewhere in Siberia, far from the North Pole.

Ocean temperatures beneath the Polar Ice Cap are a constant 28 degrees F in winter. Seals, Polar Bears, and other aquatic life thrive there. The Arctic Sea is a massive heat-source compared to the icy winds above, and provides a haven for shipwrecked sailors who wear watertight survival suits, which each of us kept in our lockers.

The Eskimos do not normally catch colds, tuberculosis, or pneumonia because germs and viruses do not thrive well there. Our guidelines were to avoid contact with Eskimos as much as possible.

Major assets to surviving in the arctic are large body size, and high fat content. That may explain why mammals smaller than a fox cannot survive above ground. It may also explain why Eskimos try to fatten up before winter, and eat pure blubber all winter long.

Ice fog is a danger to watch out for. Unlike ordinary fog, which is made up of condensed water vapor, ice fog is made up of microscopic ice crystals that have formed from water vapor without going through the liquid phase. It can form when temperatures are 20 degrees below zero. The hazard arises from the optical distortion in sunlight, in which the crystals may look like solid ice, or packed snow, hiding whatever is below it.

Not all weather phenomena are a threat to safety in Alaska. One of the loveliest sights in the Arctic is a mist called Sea Smoke. It spirals upward above large ice fields, and appears pale blue until the sun hits it. Then it bursts into all the colors of the rainbow. Many, like dust devils, can occur at the same time.

Surviving a shipwreck in Alaskan waters requires, first of all, being able to reach shore.
Once on shore, building a fire and drying out is critical. The next objective would be to find food. Fortunately, the Yukon and Klondike tributaries provide fishing opportunities all year.
Arctic Grayling, Burbot, Inconnu, and trout can be found in most streams not frozen over.
Animals are also abundant. In 1943, Alaska and the Yukon Territory were home to a million Caribou, 55,000 Moose, 50,000 Dahl Sheep, 10,000 Black Bear, 6,000 Grizzlies, and 4,000 Wolves. Ptarmigan, Grey Jays, and Ravens were also plentiful, and pine nuts were available in some areas. Our survival kits contained a large knife, a compass, fishing hooks, and matches. The rest was up to the resourcefulness of the survivor.

On a brighter note, Alaska is a land of unsurpassed beauty. The towering majesty of its mountains lures those of adventurous spirit to live and hunt in the backcountry. People still pan for gold in areas around Fairbanks and Dawson City, which have produced 13 million ounces of gold since 1885.

But the negatives of living there pile up. The first frost comes in late August, and the last one in late May, which leaves only three months above freezing. Isolation from other cities can be a burden to cope with. But the biggest negative for most could be the months of twilight that can drive some people insane. Just ask anyone who lives there and they will proclaim how much they love it--irrefutable proof that they are stark-raving mad.

Before I Forget

Thermodynamic Miracle

It is that time of year when Oklahoma becomes a land of many clouds but little rain. The last cold front from the north has long since passed through, leaving the hot Dog Days of Summer bearing down with little mercy. Wispy cirrus layers, many thousands of feet from Earth are a common sight, but they bring no rain. Blankets of stratus clouds, as motionless as concrete, sometimes spread out to cover the entire sky, but they too produce no rain. Hot winds blowing off the High Plains of the West carry little moisture into our part of the world. It has always been so.

I can remember my Dad's anxiety as his corn and cotton crops began to wilt in the heat of July and August. Each day cumulus clouds would pop up to stir new hopes of rain. All day they would float overhead, then disappear at sundown to leave a clear night sky. Day Clouds my father called them – just empty teasers for a parched land. But God, in His infinite wisdom and mercy, provided a way for rain to fall even in the hottest days of an Oklahoma summer.

His marvelous plan is a thermodynamic masterpiece of nature called the "thunderstorm".

The thunderstorm begins with a single cumulus cloud rising above a hot spot on the Earth, which becomes large enough to become a "Mother Cell". This cell, fed by moisture brought up by southern winds, is at first just another thermal updraft floating in the wind. It mysteriously begins to grow and push upward above the dew point, causing moisture to condense at an accelerated rate. Just as evaporation produces cooling, condensation produces heat (80 calories per gram). As more moisture condenses into clouds more heat is released causing more moisture-laden air to rise and a chain reaction takes place. The cloud-mass explodes upward, reaching to the "Frost Line" – 8 to 10 miles up. The updraft can reach 100 miles per hour with a core diameter of 2 to 5 miles. At that stage, the cell has become a full-blown thunderstorm. It's rising droplets of moisture hurl past the freezing level and coalesce into rain and hail.

When the condensate has become too heavy to be supported by the updraft the deluge begins.

The downward rush of precipitation drags large quantities of air with it. A cold downdraft is created right in the middle of the hot updraft. The ensuing battle of the vertical winds creates massive turbulence and the thunder and lightening of the thundercloud. Negative ions are stripped, by friction, from the churning raindrops causing the clouds to become negatively charged with the Earth becoming the positive pole. The voltaic cell can build to millions of volts and be released in flashes of lightening at 50,000 degrees F. Usually in a matter of minutes the downdraft begins to overpower the updraft and the cell becomes self-quenching. At our latitude the process seldom lasts longer than 40 minutes.

As the updraft diminishes the downdraft increases hurling vast quantities of cool air across the face of the Earth. These are the surface winds that do most of the damage. At speeds of 50 – 60 miles per hour they race outward ahead of the storm kicking up new cells which can become offspring of the mother cloud. Like a Banyan Tree new cells leapfrog across the world until the Thermodynamic engine exhausts itself, the Earth cools and the barometer returns to normal.

In farm country we welcomed the sounds of thunder and the flash of lightening of an approaching summer storm. The first flutter of tree leaves and the smell of rain were answers to a farmer's prayer. At the last moment, we kids would race for the shelter of our hay barn, snuggled up with our old hound dog and settle in to enjoy the Glories of the storm.

Jerusalem

From the first day I started riding ships one of my goals was to visit Jerusalem. That ancient and strategic city, built more than 4000 years ago by the Canaanites and conquered from the Jebusites by King David in 1004 BC, was in our Christian heritage the "Holy City of God". It became the capital of David's kingdom and his son Solomon built the first temple there. Hezekiah, Zedekiah and other Judean kings enlarged and fortified its boundaries and built an underground water supply called Hezekiah's Tunnel, which made the city practically impregnable to invaders. Sennacherib tried to conquer it but failed. But in 586 BC God let Nebuchadnezzar overrun the city and carry away its people.

The captivity ended in 538 BC when Xerxes, king of Persia, permitted the Jews to return and rebuild the city. Other conquerors came and went – the Romans, the Egyptians, the Turks and finally the British, who established Israel as an independent state in 1948.

We arrived in Haifa right at the end of the war to deliver food and supplies to a hungry people. My co-workers agreed to cover my work duties while the ship was in port, leaving me free to go wherever I wanted. As soon as we were tied up to the dock, I was off to the train station for a long and tedious uphill ride to the Holy City.

The narrow-gage train was older than anything I had seen before. Seating was on benches along the outside walls but only about half the people could sit down. Some brought their food, their coffee maker and their goats for what I expected to be a two-hour ride. That estimate was before we left the station. Once underway it became obvious that our top speed might max out at about 25 miles per hour. But the train frequently slowed to a walk on the hills. People boarded and de-boarded the train without any need to stop. Calls of nature were attended to by stepping off the train, finding a place to hide (if there was one), and then stepping back on the train while it was still in motion. People were friendly and some shared their food with me, which I accepted. It was Jewish flat bread; goat jerky and coffee served in tine cups and had the

consistency of crude oil. One sip was enough to put my nerves on edge. I discretely dumped it out the window.

Once settled into the King David Hotel I engaged a guide to show me around for a couple of days. He showed up at daybreak the next morning in a worn out old taxi – ready to go.

Our first stop was the Church of the Nativity in Bethlehem. The church was outwardly unimpressive. Built or restored in 530 AD it was a typical rock structure put together with little mortar. It contained a large courtyard where people gathered. Pilgrims were camped nearby with their tents, camels, goats and sheep. Police were everywhere. We entered through a small door, removed our shoes and hat and were guided down a long colonnade hall to a stairway leading down to the crypt where the Manger once stood. It was a humbling experience to stand in the presence of the birthplace of Christ. We paused for prayer then moved on to let others in.

From Bethlehem, which is only a few miles south of Jerusalem, we skirted the Kedron Valley and picked up the serpentine road leading down to the Dead Sea. Bathing facilities were there for tourists' convenience – for those who wanted to "float" on the water. I rented a bathing suit, walked out into the water and lay on my back like a log, floating on the surface. The heat was stifling. At 1300 feet below sea

Before I Forget

level – the lowest place on Earth – I didn't stay long. Water from the Jordan River, flowing into the Dead Sea, balances the evaporation such that the sea level is fairly constant. Salt and borax plants were along the north shore.

Our next stop was Jericho and the famous well, which was still in use. The mouth of the well is approximately 20 feet across with the walls tapering down like a cone to the water several feet below. A narrow stairway, without handrails, spirals down the wall to the water level. Getting water appeared to be both tedious and dangerous and a job for the very young.

We left Jericho and headed inland to the older cities of Ephraim, Bethel and Emmaus on our way back to Jerusalem. The countryside did not look like the "Promised Land".

The old walled city of Jerusalem covers only about 220 acres.

The narrow streets and alleys were best navigated on foot because many of the shrines and temples were not accessible by car. The Jaffa Gate (the main entrance), rebuilt by Suleiman in 1538, displayed the fortress mentality of the original builders. The entrance had a right angle turn to prevent mounted horsemen from riding through and was low enough to force a rider to dismount. I was told that all eleven gates were built like that.

From the Jaffa Gate, we walked down David Street toward the Temple Mount and the Wailing Wall.

Only Jews were permitted near the Wall, which was a place of prayer. However, the Temple Mount was accessible and we were able to tour the Dome of the Rock and other mosques in the area.

We next moved to trace the Way of the Cross, the Via Dolorosa, which leads to the site of the Crucifixion. It begins at the Lion's Gate on the eastern wall, and runs through the Muslin Quarter, and up the hill to the Church of the Holy Sepulcher. The 14 stations of Christ's suffering are marked in stone. We joined a crowd of worshipers who were singing praises in many languages. In turn we entered the church in small groups to observe the hole in the rock where the cross was planted, and finally entered the Tomb where Jesus lay. The slab of stone that was his bed was worn down by the lips of worshipers over the centuries. The experience was overwhelming. We knelt to pray with people of different religions and of different faiths, but we all prayed together.

Trip to Damascus

We arrived in Damascus about 10 AM after a tortuous two hour drive from Beirut. The road wound over the mountains of Lebanon, through the Bekaa Valley, then followed the Barada River which flows into Damascus from the west. I was expecting to see another arid city in the middle of the desert, but was pleasantly surprised. Damascus is surrounded by a rich, fertile valley comprising the Ghouta Oasis and several hundred square miles of irrigated farmland. Fields of barley, cotton and maize were intermingled with fruit trees and vegetables of many types. Water from the Barada and Awash rivers were divided and re-divided to form irrigation canals over a wide area. It was easy to see why Damascus is the most continuously inhabited city in the world, and the most frequently overrun. Strategically located on the north-south trade routes to Egypt and Jerusalem, Damascus was a hub of commerce worth fighting for. Nestled between the Lebanon Mountains and the Syrian Steppe, it is the Grand Oasis of the Desert.

Syria, which had just become independent in 1946, was very friendly to strangers. The reason for my visit was to see the place where the Apostle Paul spent three days of blindness in the house of Judas (Acts 9:11) after he met Jesus on the road. We entered the main east-west thoroughfare, called the "Street Called Straight", and threaded our way toward the center of the city. Crowds of people with their camels and goats made progress slow. The driver was constantly sounding the horn, which was ignored. At last we reached the Shrine designated as the place where the apostle stayed. A crowd of people was waiting in line to go in. I joined them. We were led, in groups of four, down a narrow stairway several feet below street level into a tiny room, which was poorly lit. The guide gave his account of Paul's experience, which closely followed the Biblical story. It was impressive that the Christian shrine was so well maintained in a Muslim country.

After a brief stay in the room we were returned to the street and invited to visit local souvenir shops, which also served food. I sampled Falafel – a local favorite – and their very black coffee.

Before heading back to Beirut we drove around the Old City and stopped at a sword shop. For nearly a thousand years Damascus Steel made the finest swords in the world. The distinctive variegated pattern produced by mixing hard and soft steels in thin layers was not only beautiful, but produced a hard-tough cutting edge which was superior to the high-carbon steels of the day. How the sword makers of Damascus gained such profound knowledge of making swords, in such an unlikely place, is unknown. The process, still in use today, produced expensive swords primarily for export. They were well out of my price range.

Back in Beirut the cab driver decided to double his price. I really didn't mind. If the price had been four times as much I would have gone anyway. It was an opportunity to witness an important bit of Biblical history that I could not pass up.

Before I Forget

The Engineering Curse

I first heard the term in a physics class at the University of Oklahoma. It was used to define a situation where two objectives appeared to be mutually exclusive. In that situation the engineer's job is to expand the technology to minimize the differences.

Real-life examples abound. Even the pyramid builders made engineering changes as they went along. For example, the slant angle of pyramids built in the Fourth Dynasty tended to be 43 degrees. In the Sixth Dynasty the angle was increased to 51 degrees and 52 minutes. Although stability may have been a consideration, it may have been as simple as giving the structure a more pleasing appearance.

Cathedral builders faced a similar curse in determining how to build rock structures to great heights and keep them stable. They learned by trial and error that massive lateral thrusts of arches and domes are concentrated one third of the way up the curvature. At that point a counter-acting force must be applied to make the structure stable. It took 400 years to move from the low-heavy Romanesque designs of the First Millennium (with 60 foot ceilings) to the soaring light-weight structures of French Gothic that produced the masterpieces such as Notre Dame, Chartres, Cologne and others of the Renaissance Period, with ceiling heights up to 160 feet. These changes were made possible by the development of the ribbed vault, the pointed arch and the flying buttress.

The builders of wooden sailing ships faced their own curse – how to build hulls strong enough to prevent "hogging", an upward bend in the keel, which adversely affected both speed and controllability. Ships used for great explorations – by Columbus, Magellan and others – were small by modern standards. Steel was needed to solve that problem.

In our lifetime we have witnessed, to a large extent, the reduction of the load vs. range curse imposed upon airplanes. In its infancy the maximum range for a commercial airplane was believed to be 750 miles no matter how big, or how many engines the plane had. The unbending laws of physics seemed to dictate that two-thirds of a plane's horsepower would be required to life the airframe into the air. Of the remaining third, half was required to carry the fuel, leaving only a sixth of the horsepower to carry the payload. Range vs. payload seemed to be mutually exclusive.

With the advent of World War II things began to change. Engines became lighter and more powerful, external struts were removed, wheels were retracted, rivets were made flush, air frames were streamlined, and wing loading was increased from the 2.5 pounds per square foot ---used by Orville Wright – to 70 pounds per square foot for the Douglas DC-3 in 1940. The DC-3 became the world's first truly efficient airplane and had a range of 1300 miles.

Later I have discovered an engineering curse of my own. Sitting in my easy chair and mowing the lawn seem to be mutually exclusive objectives. The immutable laws of physics say that I cannot be in two places at the same time, which means that I have a choice. Choices, of course, should not be made quickly.

So, for now, I will enjoy my iced tea and ponder what other curses I might ignore.

A Strange Confrontation

Two pairs of geese brought their hatchlings to feed on our lot, next to the lake, each morning. The little balls of fur would scatter in all directions as their parents watched. The ganders were on constant alert, always with their heads up.

One morning just after daybreak, they came ashore just as a large raccoon was heading home for the day. The raccoon seemed not to notice the goslings as he plodded along the waterfront, but the ganders immediately went on the attack. With wings flapping, necks bowed, and honking loudly they met the raccoon head-on. After a flurry of activity the raccoon retreated up a nearby tree. After a few minutes the raccoon started back down to go on his way, but the ganders were on him before he hit the ground. So, back up the tree he went. The geese then seemed to ignore him and moved on in their feeding. The raccoon held his position in the tree for about 15 minutes, then he ran out on a limb, jumped to the ground and scurried off in his original direction in a wide circle around the geese. They didn't seem to notice as he disappeared into the woods.

If all parents would show as much concern for the welfare of their offspring as geese do, this would be a better world.

Gordon Thompson

The Last Reunion

Joy Consolidated Country School graduated its last senior class in 1943 – my class of six. For sixty-five years some of us have been returning to celebrate our heritage in that abandoned place, now empty and crumbling. The numbers have gotten smaller each year. This year, the remnant of all those who passes this way was down to little more than a dozen - those who have managed to weather the storms of time. None of my classmates made it. The meeting carried a note of sadness because of those who have passed on, and knowing that this would be the last time we would meet together.

We talked about our kids, our jobs and the fortunes and misfortunes of life. Some bore emotional scars engraved in their faces. Others managed a smile, or a laugh or two; but for most of us it was difficult to hold back the tears. That old schoolhouse was fundamental to our heritage. And to see it crumbling was as if the memories and traditions of a lifetime were crumbling with it. It was a grim reminder that my generation has already passed with what legacy we would leave essentially complete.

Where did the time go? It seems to have passed without making a sound. Each of us made our footprints in the sands of time according to the gifts that God gave us – tempered by the laws of chance, and dominated by our own desires and wishes.

I am afraid that my footprints barely show, and perhaps only God can see them.

Reflections on Being Poor

I can recall with some nostalgia the days of my youth down in southern Oklahoma near the little town of Wynnewood. Dad was a sharecropper working worn-out land as a cotton farmer. His wealth consisted of two teams of horses, a wagon, some farm tools an old Model T Ford truck, and seven kids. We were very poor – if only a lack of funds defined the condition. We were poor if the absence of spending money made us unhappy or angry at the world. Neither applied to us.

Poverty has many forms. No one is poor if he can see the gold in the rising sun or the silver in a full moon. No one is poor who can drift off to sleep listening to the croaking of bullfrogs in a farm pond and not worry about tomorrow. Those of us who lived with the rich aroma of nature all around us had no definition for poverty.

We believed that no one is poor who knows the great riches of close friendships or the treasure of a loving family.

Poverty, in all its forms, is not inherited. Everyone must buy his own. In the final analysis, no amount of wealth – whether earned or received as a gift – can fill an emptiness of the Soul.

Gordon Thompson

Remembering the Weather

One of the frequent questions asked on ships is "What is the weather going to do today?" Talk of fronts and air masses has long been common among land-based peoples, but reading the changes in weather becomes more important for ships at sea.

Vilhelm Bjerknes, Norwegian physicist, developed the air-mass concept in use today. He discovered the simple truth that weather moves around the Earth in great waves thousands of miles apart. He discovered that air circulates in distinct chunks with definite boundaries, with little or no mixing at the edges. His theory explains how a warm soggy night can suddenly be replaced by a cool crisp morning, and why winter comes in packets of a few days at a time.

Some air masses are defined as the Polar Canadian Front, which sweeps down from the north, and the Tropical Gulf Front, which sweeps up through the Mississippi Valley, bringing vast amounts of moisture with it. Tropical Pacific Fronts – from both directions – compete for dominance as the seasons change.

Air masses, like wines, can sometimes be recognized by their color and taste by those who spend much time at sea. Some seem smoky, some glassy green and some crystal clear. Some smell of peat moss, some of pine forests and some smell of dust and sand. Each combination of humidity, warmth, dryness and coolness can be encountered, each with its own dew point and halo around the moon. Labrador and Siberian air masses come in chunks of millions of cubic miles, take days to pass, and the smells may change from day to day.

Some meteorological mysteries make no sense. Death Valley, located 36 degrees north of the equator, is the hottest place on earth – sometimes reaching 134 degrees F. The coldest place in the Northern Hemisphere is located 27 degrees south of the North Pole in the mountains of Siberia. Elevation seems to control.

On the average more cloud cover occurs at sea than over land. The Southern Hemisphere is cloudier than the Northern. But perhaps strangest of all – the Sahara Desert may have more clouds than occur in the cloud-vacuum of the Horse Latitudes, which is located in the middle of the ocean.

How fortunate we are that most clouds occur in polar frontal areas where most of the world's population lives. Bjerknes called this belt of continuous conflict between different air masses the "Great Air War", without which there would be little rain. This delicate balance of the meteorological scales is, without doubt, all part of God's Plan.

Gordon Thompson

Riding the Bumble-Bee

Sometimes I think that flying is not meant for man. Our ship was heading west in Mid Pacific when suddenly a twin-engine C-47 cargo plane approached from the west, limping along on one engine. It circled slowly, as if to land in the ocean where we could rescue whomever was aboard. But rough seas and a brisk wind made a water landing risky. So after one circle it continued eastward. The nearest land was more than a thousand miles away. Their chances of reaching safety were slim.

Lindberg pioneered transoceanic flying in a land-based plane at a time when the odds were only 500 to 1 that his single-engine plane would make it. He had considered using two engines, as the French were doing, but decided against it. The added weight of the engine and its fuel would introduce the possibility that the plane would crash if either engine failed. God was with him.

The question then arose – how many engines are enough to insure safety? Would two, three, four or six be adequate? Endurance tests showed that a piston aircraft engine of that period might fail once in 6000 hours. With four engines running independently, the largest number deemed practicable, failure of one would be survivable – even if safety were hundreds of miles away. That decision proved to be a good one. During and after World War II there is no record of a four-engine plane being lost at sea from multiple engine failure. Separate ignition and fuel systems proved to be remarkably reliable.

So why am I uncomfortable flying in this modern age of jet engines which never seem to fail? I call it the "Bumblebee" effect. When I look around and see 400 other people on the plane with me, and 500 tons of aircraft, my engineering instincts scream "THIS THING WON'T FLY".

I remember a moment of panic as we readied for takeoff from Honolulu in a 747 at night. I couldn't believe the number of

Before I Forget

people crowded into the narrow seats. I turned on the cockpit microphone to listen to the pilots, and got this shocking news:

"This is United too heavy---- Ready for takeoff".

How was I to know that he was telling the tower
"This is Heavy Aircraft, United, Flight 2, ready for take-off."

When I'm riding on a bumblebee, there are some things I had rather not know.

Gordon Thompson

Edible Obnoxious Weeds

When I was growing up Grandmother Sims always had some strange looking vegetables for us to eat. Things she learned from local Indians who never planted a garden, but always had greens in their diet. Mother picked up the tradition and we boys were often sent off on a weed hunt to find Lambs Quarter, pigweed, and purslane – all of which can be eaten raw. All are as nutritious as spinach and grow about every place you don't want them.

The reason nobody grows them for food probably has to do with the way they look. All look like obnoxious weeds with various degrees of repulsiveness built in. The pigweed is a scraggy-fuzzy leafed tall plant with a whitish fuzz-ball seedpod on top. Colored bluish-green with white dust all over it, it is the last thing you would think of eating. But if you are hungry you can pull it up and eat stalk and all. It tastes a little like rhubarb and about as fibrous. Lambs Quarter looks more like spinach and grows up to six feet tall. We would cut huge armloads and feed it to the hogs. They loved it. Purslane was more rare and found mostly near water or streams. It had a red stalk and little roundish slick leaves that look more poisonous than edible.

Mother was embarrassed that our family had to scrounge for food like that, but it was just another food source – like squirrel, rabbit and crawdads from the ponds.

It is such a waste that no one eats them anymore.

Premium Pay

I earned my way through the University of Oklahoma by working as a crewmember on merchant ships during the summer months. When spring finals were over I would head out to Baltimore or down to Houston to catch a ship to Europe or Asia. I looked for ships carrying hazardous cargo because of the premium pay.

One summer I took a job on an old Liberty ship which was being loaded in Houston. The premium pay was very good. When I arrived for duty it was obvious why the extra pay was needed – raw sulphur was being loaded. A yellow dust cloud covered everything. The crew was wearing masks, safety goggles and protective clothing. I put on similar gear and joined them.

In a manner of hours, loading was completed and we headed out to sea bound for London. By the time we had cleared the Florida Keys all four cargo bays were on fire from spontaneous combustion. This often occurs when sulphur comes in contact with rusted steel. Sulphur burns with a quarter-inch high blue flame and melts the adjourning sulphur – all of which floats on water. Fire hoses were useless. The Standard Operation Procedure for such emergencies is to seal up the fire as tight as possible, constantly flush the decks with water to keep them cool, and let it burn. We were drawing 33 feet of water with a top speed of 8.5 knots. The trip to London would take 22 days.

It proved to be impossible to seal out the sulphur dust and toxic fumes from our eyes, nose and throat in the course of eating, bathing and sleeping. By the end of the first week, our eyes were badly swollen and we could hardly talk. When we finally arrived in London, ambulances were waiting to take us to the hospital. The fires were blanketed with foam and the sulphur was pneumatically removed.

The premium pay wasn't worth it.

Gordon Thompson

Christmas Shoes

I had just turned 8 years old before the Christmas of 1932. The Depression had hit our family hard that year. Dad's cotton crop brought barely enough to pay our grocery bill with nothing left over for the other necessities. Mother made shirts for me and my brother and dresses for my two sisters to wear to school. But our winter shoes were always ordered from the Sears catalog, to arrive at Christmas time. After going barefoot all summer and into the fall, we were excited for what Christmas would bring.

On Christmas Eve we gathered around our pot-bellied stove to eat popcorn and homemade candy and to open our gifts. As I was putting on my beautiful new boots, which had a knife pocket on the side, Dad was preparing to go out into the cold to feed the livestock. A light snow had fallen and Dad was taking extra care to cover the holes in the soles of his shoes. He carefully cut the tongue from each shoe, placed it inside to cover the hole, then cut a piece of cardboard to fit over the leather. As I watched him do that the joy of having new boots suddenly vanished. For the first time in my life I became aware of the sacrifices Mother and Dad were making for us.

The shoes my parents gave us that year were not just "Christmas presents". They were a gift of love that has stayed embedded in my memory through the years.

Gordon Thompson

The Money Counter

Just fresh out of high school and waiting to be drafted into the Army, I took a summer job on a small dairy farm to replace a helper who had joined the Navy. John and Maggie McDaniels, whose daughters were married and gone, were struggling to stay in the dairy business, which required hard work and long hours.

When John came looking for a helper he was a friendly and likeable guy who was also fun to be around. I liked him immediately and signed on for the summer at $15 per week, plus room and board. My bunk was in the dairy room, which houses the walk-in icebox and a milk separator. My closet consisted of two nails on the wall and a cardboard box on the floor. But it was adequate for my needs, since I would spend precious little time there.

Our routine was simple – up at 4 AM, milk cows, separate the cream and store it in the icebox, feed the horses, then stop for breakfast. After breakfast it was off to sickle-mow his large alfalfa field with horse-drawn equipment. John would lead off with his mower and I would follow with mine. We usually kept a steady pace until noon. After lunch John became increasingly lethargic, and by 2 or 3 PM he would stop his mower wherever he happened to be and announce to me that he "had to go count his money". With that, he would leave his team and mower where it happened to be and walk away – always in the direction of Wynnewood, about two miles away. I cut his team loose to return to the barn and continued mowing until milking time at sundown. John never returned to help me with the milking and feeding chores.

It was well after dark when I would go in for supper. Maggie always had plenty of food on the table but was nowhere to be seen. I ate alone, then plopped into bed for some instant sleep. I was awakened sometime in the night by Maggie dragging John in from the car. There was no fighting, scolding, or angry words. Suddenly there was only the silence of the night. The next day it would be repeated all over again. John was an alcoholic.

We had nearly finished the mowing when John stopped his mower, stepped off as usual, then promptly collapsed with severe convulsions. I thought he was dying and rushed to get Maggie with her car. When Maggie saw him she fell to her knees and broke into uncontrollable sobs. She whispered a prayer as we placed him in the car.

The Pauls Valley Hospital was 10 miles away. The diagnoses was "Delirium-tremens" caused by acute alcoholism. He was placed in detox for an indefinite time, and never returned to his farm while I was there.

After all these years I can still hear him say "Carry on, Son. I've got to go count my money," as he headed into town.

Gordon Thompson

The 'Possum Eaters

During my teen years cousin Calvin and I hunted possum and skunks in the winter months for the pelts. That is how we earned spending money and bought our clothes. After harvesting the pelts we sold the carcasses to the Negro families in Wynnewood for 25 cents each.

One customer, who was feeding seven children, often bragged about how good baked possum was. As veteran eaters of about everything that flew, swam or crawled, we figured that eating a possum would be just another notch in our culinary belt.

We selected a large fat one for our first try. After baking for an hour we were shocked at how much grease had to be drained off. We added sweet potatoes and baked for another hour, then sat down for a possum feast.

The meat turned out to be a dark red, grease-saturated stringy mess. I looked at Calvin, who had turned a dull shade of gray, and he looked at me – probably the same color – daring each other to go first. Neither of us could back down so we dug in.

Like most wild game the taste was extremely bland and totally dominated by the taste of the fat, which also had an unpleasant odor. We gagged our way through a few bites, hoping the other would throw in the towel. By mutual agreement we abandoned the experiment and fed the whole thing to the dogs.

When word got out a school that we had eaten a possum you can guess what happened – for a time we were called the "Possum Eaters".

The Truck Ride

During World War II hitchhiking was a reliable way to get around for those of us who didn't have a car. When Vought Aircraft in Dallas started advertising for workers, Sister's husband Raymond asked me to go with him for an interview. We walked over to US 77, a half-mile from our house, and caught a grocery truck to Dallas.

The interview line was long and slow. By the time we got back on the highway to come home the sun was going down. But luck was with us. A farmer picked us up and carried us to the "Y" where Hwy 82 turns east to Sherman. He let us off and wished us well.

It was a lonely place with nothing but scrubland in all directions. A chill was in the air and traffic was slow. At midnight we were still there, shivering on the side of the road and praying for a kind hearted soul to come along.

About 2 AM a set of bouncing headlights appeared along with the guttural roar of a diesel engine running at the max. Raymond held out his thumb – not expecting a truck traveling at such high speed to stop. However, when the driver saw us, he slammed on his brakes and by burning rubber was almost able to stop. As he slid by he yelled, "Jump in the back".

We raced to catch up and hand-vaulted up to land in a sitting position on the truck bed – a maneuver we often used to board Dad's old hay truck. To our great surprise we splashed down into about two inches of fresh cow manure, a smelly lubricant that had us sliding along on our backs. Raymond rolled to one side; I rolled to the other. As we grabbed the sideboards to keep from being ejected out the back, the driver had his engine screaming for acceleration.

We made our way up behind the cab to get protection from the chilling wind, but found none. Within half an hour we were climbing the little Arbuckle Range which slowed our speed a little and gave brief respite from the cold. Once he crested the high point, and a couple of hairpin curves, the driver rolled down into the Washita River Valley at full throttle. We could easily have been doing 100 miles per hour. The cow manure now caked and drying, was our only wind barrier, and probably kept us from freezing to death.

As we approached our drop point we banged on the cab to let the driver know we wanted off. At the last moment he slammed his brakes. Again there was screeching and burning of rubber, but the truck never completely stopped. We heard him yell, "Jump off!" as we tumbled on the side of the road and lay there wondering if we had any broken bones.

About 4 AM we sneaked into Dad's hayloft and buried ourselves in the hay to get warm. But 4 AM was Dad's getting-up time and he soon found us – hiding like a couple of whipped dogs. He immediately called for Mother to come and see – the last thing we wanted. Mother took one look and burst out laughing. She laughed until tears rolled down her cheeks – no one could out-laugh my mother.

Nearly 60 years later we were visiting Sis and Raymond at their home near Duncan. Raymond was ill with cancer. I found him sitting in his big chair, emaciated and weak. I knelt beside his chair not knowing what to say. He looked at me and a smile flickered across his face.

"Do you remember that truck ride from Dallas?"

I nodded trying not to laugh.

"That driver sure pulled a good one on us, didn't he?"

"Yes", I said. "He gave a couple of Hobos the ride of their lives and probably laughed all the way to Oklahoma City."

Before I Forget

The Swimming Hole

In our teen years cousin Calvin and I were frequent visitors to a spring-fed stock pond on the Wolf Ranch. It was the least polluted swimming hole within our walking range, and a favorite recreation place for local families. It was located deep inside the ranch, which contained many cattle, a mean Hereford bull, several mares and a stallion. The stallion was never a threat but the bull was easily disturbed and had to be avoided at all costs.

On a hot Saturday in August we headed for the swimming hole for a refreshing swim. To get to the pond we had to cross an open prairie which had no trees except for a clump of Black Jack Oaks used for shade. Jack Oaks, as we called them, are a small oak, which is genetically programmed to shed its small branches in times of drought. The limbs die and turn black, but remain attached to the tree for years. In time the trees take on a black appearance from all the dead limbs, and more closely resemble a thorn bush than a tree. Climbing one is generally unthinkable.

We arrived at the stock pond to find it nearly dry from lack of rain. But to our delight dozens of large carp could be seen swimming in the shallow water. Without hesitation we stripped off our clothes and began to catch the fish by hand and toss them on the bank. In a few minutes we had several weighing a total of about 25 pounds, which we strung on a wire to carry home. We were so covered with mud we couldn't put our clothes on so we headed across the prairie naked, with the fish swinging between us.

We scanned the prairie for the bull but saw only the stallion and his mares grazing a great distance off our intended path. We thought that we didn't have a worry in the world. But when we drew abreast of their position, the stallion suddenly became very agitated. While looking in our direction he began to snort and paw the ground, a signal we recognized as an imminent attack on whatever was bothering him, namely us or our smelly fish. Instinctively we dropped our fish and ran flat-out for the nearest cover, which happened to be the clump of Jack Oaks. Left with no other choice we gritted our teeth and began the painful climb. Neither of us made it more than six feet from the ground, but fortunately for us horses never seem to look up. So he never saw us. We sat there, bleeding from our wounds until he rejoined the mares. The decent, we found, was as painful as the climb.

When the horses moved away we headed home dreading embarrassment which was sure to come. We stopped at our water well to wash off the mud and blood, hoping no medical attention would be needed. But no luck there. We each had several lacerations, which would require Mother's expert doctoring. We headed home to face the "music".

The "music" turned out to be Mother's uncontrollable laughter as she applied rubbing alcohol to our wounds. She could hardly wait to tell her sister Ada, Calvin's mother, and the rest of the community as well. As the story spread our injuries were exaggerated, both in severity and location to the point that some folks wondered if our posterity was in jeopardy. We also became the butt of jokes and "knowing" looks at school. After all, who would be stupid enough to climb a Black Jack-naked?

As I recall that was our last trip to our favorite swimming hole.

A Rabbit Hunt

Our culture in southern Oklahoma included hunting to supplement our food supply in the wintertime. We harvested rabbits and squirrels as naturally as we butchered hogs and chickens. We killed to eat but never just for sport, and we never killed anything while it was eating. As Baptists, eating was a sacred ritual that should not be disturbed.

I had been on many rabbit hunts before and enjoyed the chase. Contrary to what many people believe, rabbits don't run flat-out all the time when chased. They sprint to get ahead of the dogs, then adjust their speed for endurance, just to stay out of reach. Our old dog loved to chase rabbits but could never get close enough to catch one. They baying of an old hound defined the spirit of the chase and was what hunters lived for.

One day in October I took our dog and was wandering across the prairies of the Wolf Ranch. The ranch contained several prairies, some nearly a mile square, separated by timbered streamlets that contained water only when it rained.

Rabbits prefer open grassland for nesting and spend most of their time there. As we neared a heavily grassed area a large rabbit jumped from his hiding place – and the chase was on.

He sprinted away, quickly putting distance between himself and the dog. The chase turned eastward across an open space that stretched for half a mile. To stay clear of the timber, the rabbit turned south toward an adjacent prairie, then west for the beginning of a huge circle which would eventually bring him back to his starting point. I sat down to wait.

The chase went on for half an hour, sometimes nearly out of earshot, before heading back in my direction. He headed straight for me, apparently unaware that I was there. Only a few feet from where I was sitting he flopped down on his side breathing heavily. I would never shoot a helpless animal while it was lying down, so my plan was to give him a little time to recover, then I would stand up. He would surely take off running, and I would give him 20 yards head start before I pulled the trigger.

I stood up and walked toward the rabbit expecting him to jump and run. The rabbit didn't move. He just looked at me as it to say, "I've gone as far as I can go – do whatever you wish." The dog was then approaching slowly on the trail so I reached down and picked the rabbit up by the hind legs and cradled him in my arms. He made no effort to get away. I could tell that he was old and underweight. His coat seemed thin and tattered. He had run a good race and deserved to be free. I held the dog's collar and turned the rabbit loose.

God placed the rabbit on the bottom of the food chain where dogs, coyotes, owls, hawks and people desire to eat them. Their only defense is excellent eyesight, a superb ability to run and a desire to live.

I was glad to see him go.

Oklahoma Weather

There is a saying here, that if you don't like the weather, just wait an hour or two and it will change. This derives from our position (35 degrees N), which frequently straddles the Jet Stream that often swings down from Canada. Warm and cold fronts are integral components of the regular metabolism of the sky, and take their turn in disturbing the tranquility of the land.

Cold fronts are the most spectacular. Shaped like a boot with a rounded toe protruding forward, followed by a foot sloping upward to the frost-line, the cold front rolls along the ground and wedges beneath warmer air in its path. As the warm air is lifted up, rows of beautiful thunderclouds form like dancing balls of cotton. A broad bank may form with bursts of rain, but usually only for a short time. In a matter of minutes the cold front has swallowed the entire sky.

Warm fronts are entirely different. Days before its arrival high-flying cirrus clouds, called Mare's Tails, herald the slow moving warm air, which approaches nose-up. The leading edge rides high, like a ski pointed upward. This ski-shaped air mass, with its tail dragging the ground may be a thousand miles long. Such a large mass is longer in coming and longer in going than the snappy cold.

Apart from local thunderstorms which dot the landscape in the heat of summer, alternating warm and cold fronts come and go in unending procession to define and punctuate the seasons of the year. Some fronts are strong, some are weak and some have no definable boundaries. But they keep on coming in a predictable rhythm that provides the land with the water it needs to make it habitable for man and beast.

The thermodynamics of the atmosphere that makes this possible are all part of God's Plan.

Gordon Thompson

A Friendly Banker

When I was very young my father was farming a little place south of Wynnewood, Oklahoma and struggling to feed his large family. Each spring at planting time it was Dad's custom to borrow a hundred dollars to tide us over until harvest time in the fall.

Once Dad took me along on the trip to the bank so I could learn how business was transacted between grownups. We were cordially received and ushered into a small waiting room where the mortgage papers would be signed. The collateral for the loan included Dad's horses, wagon and all his farming tools. Dad didn't mind because he always paid back all he owed, and besides the banker was a trusted friend who never refused to help.

As we sat down at the table the banker explained the transaction in words something like this:
"Now, Sie (my dad), you are borrowing a hundred dollars which is to be paid back at harvest time. The interest rate is the usual 10 percent, or ten dollars, which I am holding back so you will only owe an even hundred in the fall. Do you have any questions?" Dad, who only had a third grade education, nodded that he understood and signed the note. The banker handed Dad $90 with a friendly hand shake and we left.

Years later, when I was a student at the University of Oklahoma, I remembered that transaction with shocked amazement. Dad repaid the loan in six months, yet he paid a full year's interest in advance, and received only 90 percent of the money on which the interest was charged. The true interest rate was not 10 percent, but a whopping 22 percent, and my poor old Dad never knew the difference.

My father passed away in 1965 still believing the banker was his friend.

Before I Forget

Chili Supper

For many years at Calvary Baptist Church in Clinton, Iowa I was the un-elected head cook at Fellowship Dinners. My specialties were steaks and hotcakes but I was dumb enough to try anything. So when the time came for the Father-Son Chili Supper I was asked to prepare the food – which I was glad to do. Just how hard can making chili be?

The afternoon of the planned event caught me short on time, so instead of making chili for 30 people from scratch, I decided to buy commercial containers of a popular brand, add spices and beans and no one would know the difference. The weather had been hovering around 10 degrees for several days, the significance of which never crossed my mind.

A couple of hours before time to eat I had the tables all set and everything ready to go – except the chili.

I called the grocery wholesale warehouse to have two gallons ready for quick pickup. In a few minutes I was back at the church with a big porcelain pot on the stove boiling with an inch of water in the bottom.

When I opened the first gallon can I was appalled to see that it was frozen solid. Undaunted I dumped the contents onto the counter – only to see it bounce off onto the floor and roll across the room like a rubber log. I chased it into a corner, retrieved it and placed it back on the counter. Rising to the challenge I tried chipping it into smaller pieces with knives, forks and a meat cleaver – all to no avail.

The matter was getting serious; I was running out of time.

Another brainstorm hit me. I raced home, got a hacksaw and a hatchet and returned to the task. The saw was useless, so I attacked the chili with the hatchet – swinging wildly with particles flying in all directions. But it worked, and chunks of chili went into the boiling pot in rapid succession.

I opened the second container expecting to repeat the process, when suddenly a dense cloud of acrid blue smoke filled the kitchen, the church and much of the neighborhood. I learned quickly that burned bean smoke ranks right up there with Mustard Gas as a way to rout the enemy in time of war. It was unbearable.

About that time a herd of young boys arrived, expecting to eat. Coughing and holding his noses, I heard one say, "No way will I eat that stuff, no matter what it is".

Recognizing a disaster in progress I shut down the chili operation and went out into the dining hall to apologize and offer pancakes as an alternative. My offer fell on deaf ears. En masse my 30 eaters exited the church and headed for McDonald's.

After I had cleaned the walls and ceiling of chili splatter, I headed home ashamed and dejected for having let them down. After awhile the irony of the situation hit me and I began to laugh. The gyrations I went through to produce such a fiasco were, in some respects, heroic. So what? The chili was burned and I had to throw the pot away, but the only casualties were my ego and title of Head Cook, which I didn't deserve anyway.

And strangely enough, nobody ever asked me to cook chili again.

Tricks of the Mind

It had been a poor winter for hunting furs that year. At the grownup age of 16 cousin Calvin and I were scrounging for "dating" money for a couple of cute little girls in Wynnewood. With movies costing a quarter and cokes costing a nickel, a date with a city girl could cost a dollar or more, and would soon deplete our meager reserves. The urgency of the situation forced us to hunt outside our normal area into unfamiliar territory to the east of the Wolf Ranch, and southward toward the Little Arbuckle Range. As seasoned night hunters we had no problem going wherever furs might be found.

It was a cold November night when we set out at 10 PM with our old hound, a lantern and a skinning knife in case we found anything. We planned to walk eastward a couple of miles, then circle south, then west to bring us back about daybreak. The old hound set a brisk pace as we let him follow his nose.

By 3 AM we had followed several fruitless trails and were ready to head home. A clear sky had clouded over but this was no problem. My infallible internal compass told me exactly which way to go. Calvin's infallible internal compass told him to go in the opposite direction, which brought on a heated discussion that lasted several minutes. We could hear traffic noise from US Hwy 77, which would be west: and from State Hwy 7, which would be south; and from Hwy 29, which would be north, or vice versa. We didn't know which was which.

We flipped a coin and started walking. After an hour, exhaustion was setting in and the old hound was clearly ready to quit. Then, out of nowhere, an old farmhouse appeared – where no house was supposed to be. It made no sense. As we discussed the various possibilities the old hound trotted over and lay down on the porch. We tried to call him back, but he wouldn't budge. We could not leave him there; so we had no choice but to wait for daybreak to retrieve him, then head home from wherever we happened to be. We lay down on the ground and waited.

As dawn approached I was shocked at what I saw. Dad emerged from the back door – heading out for morning chores. He spotted the hound, looked around for us, then went on toward the barn. I was too embarrassed to move. In our world, fearless hunters didn't get lost, and if they did they would never admit it – not even to themselves.

The way I saw it – WE WERE NOT LOST - we were just temporarily confused – a little trick of the mind.

Before I Forget

A Tender Farewell

A doe gave birth to two fawns in the thicket by the end of our lot. All summer they had been daily visitors. Each evening about 6 PM they ambled through on their way to bed down in the thicket for the night. Last week I witnessed a standoff with a large coyote, wherein the doe chased the coyote away from the fawns. It was a rare experience.

The fawns are now more than half grown. The spots are gone. They can run with the fastest of the herd. This evening I think I witnessed the doe saying goodbye to her babies. They appeared on our lot about
6 PM as usual. The doe frolicked and played with the fawns for nearly an hour. She nuzzled them, licked them and raced around them as if playing some game. Then she disappeared into the thicket and was gone. The fawns continued to play for several minutes, not realizing she had left. A few minutes later I saw the doe emerge from the underbrush about half a mile away running at full gallop in the direction of the forested hill where the herd often stays. She had said goodbye to her babies and was heading back to the herd for the new breeding season soon to begin.

It was a touching moment that I had to witness to believe.

Gordon Thompson

A Camel Ride

When our ship made a cargo stop in Alexandria it gave me a chance to fulfill a life-long dream of visiting the pyramids. I hopped a train to Cairo intending to rent a car, drive out to the pyramids, look all around, and be back to the ship the same day.

In Cairo my plans suddenly changed. During the war you couldn't just "rent" a car, and there were no tour buses to take you there. If you wanted to visit the pyramids the only way to get there was to walk or ride a camel. I grew up riding a plow horse, so riding a camel would be no big deal – so I thought.

At the camel stables several surprises awaited. You can't walk up to a camel, swing up into the saddle and go. African camels can be seven feet tall, and what passes for a saddle has no stirrups.

Camels also have the bad habit of biting unwanted riders. The handler carefully explained the procedure: first, he would make the camel lie down (fold); then I would slide into the saddle, grab anything I could hold onto and wait for the camel to stand up. The standing up was a big surprise. Camels are not like horses; their rear ends are the last to go down and the first to come up – a move that can pitch an unwary rider headlong into the sand. This must be a common fun thing for the camels. Once the camel was standing I was shocked at how high I was and how unstable the saddle felt. A camel's hump is not part of their bone structure. It is like a huge ball bearing that rolls around at every movement the camel makes. With no saddle-horn to hold onto, I could tell that this would not be a fun ride.

It turned out to be a long day. Camels have only two speeds – stop and slow. It was dark when we got back to Cairo and I decided to spend the night there. The nearest hotel was the Elat, probably built during the reign of Cleopatra. It had five floors, no window screens, no elevator and no air-conditioning. Also the primitive bathroom had no tub or shower. The desk clerk informed me that if I wanted to shower it would cost extra for access to the common showers on the first floor. It was a no-brainer – I didn't need a shower.

As I climbed the stairs to my room on the fifth floor I noticed that none of the occupied rooms had their doors closed. When I entered my room the reason became clear – it must have been 100 degrees in there. The hot desert winds precluded any thought of sleep until about 3 o'clock in the morning.

On the train ride back to Alexandria I was thankful for having seen the pyramids, but I was quite certain that I had had enough camel riding to last me a lifetime.

Gordon Thompson

Magic Fireplace

Everyone needs a quiet time to slow down, to contemplate and recharge emotional batteries that have run low. My time is before daybreak when the world is sleeping.

I brew the coffee, light the fireplace and sit in the darkness and let the soothing flames attend my soul. It is a medication that cannot be bought in stores. It is like an infusion of God's Spirit that covers such a multitude of sins and blots out the anxieties of the world.

From time immemorial man has gathered around fires, drawn to its relaxing aura, its life-giving warmth and its spiritual connection to The Almighty.

Fire, like water, is one of the pedestals upon which life rests and, like water, will one day destroy all.

Before I Forget

The Lighthouse

Cape Hatteras, long known as a graveyard for sailing ships, juts out on the coast of the Carolinas forming a huge bulge in the coastline. That bulge forms a springboard that deflects hurricanes away from Delaware and New Jersey, making towns like Ocean City, possible. It also deflects the Gulf Stream sending it farther eastward to the benefit of ships heading for Europe from the Gulf. But the outer finger of the Cape has an extremely low profile, which presents a "blind" hazard to shipping coming from the south. Even modern ships with radar have run aground there.

Our tanker, returning from Venezuela loaded with crude oil, picked up the Gulf Stream off Florida on our way to Philadelphia. It was a rainy night with poor visibility. Our navigator was "riding the sonar", determining our position by the depth of the water, to supplement poor signals from the radar. This meant staying within ten miles of the shore, so our sonar would work. The radio direction finder was also of little help.

We expected to clear the Cape by midnight but shortly after 11 PM our sonar alarm went off signaling shallow water. The pilot, believing that we were well clear of land, took no immediate action except to grab his binoculars and peer into the night. Almost immediately he shouted, "Hard right". He could see the Hatteras Lighthouse close-up through the storm. As the loaded tanker swung slowly to starboard, the sonar dropped toward zero. We held our breath and prayed. It was a narrow miss.

I have remembered that moment over the years, and again just recently, when I heard the song Lighthouse sung by the Florida Boys. Their words have a special meaning for me, and goes something like this:

> I thank God for the Lighthouse
> I owe my life to Him.
> Jesus is the Lighthouse, that stands there for me.

Gordon Thompson

He shines His Light around me
So I can clearly see.
If it weren't for the Lighthouse,
Where would this ship be?

Can Mother Rabbits Cry?

Our apartment sat on a hilltop overlooking the city. Our lawn was large, with many oaks and maples that provided lots of shade. It was a favorite nesting place for rabbits.

A portion of our yard was fenced-in with chicken wire for our dog. Squirrels and rabbits could come and go as they pleased and, perhaps for safety, rabbits were frequent visitors.

One morning I noticed that a mother rabbit had made a nest inside our fence and had her babies there. To protect her babies from our dog I erected a loop of fence around the nest to provide a separate little yard just for her. She could come and go as she pleased. I checked each morning to see that the babies were safe.

Things went well for about a week. Then one morning I noticed the nest had been torn out and the babies were gone. I suspected that a hungry raccoon had found them. With her babies gone I expected the mother to leave the area immediately, but she didn't.

For five days she sat quietly by the empty nest, as if in mourning, waiting for her babies to return. And one has to wonder - can mother rabbits cry?

Gordon Thompson

On Fishing

Of the many sports that I am not good at fishing tops the list. This is surprising considering that my siblings are all accomplished fisher-persons with long records of catching everything that swims. Lack of talent didn't fully explain my meager success. It had to be simple stupidity on my part, or superior smartness of the fish I was trying to catch.

Then came a report by the U.S. Fish and Wildlife Services that put me in a very poor light. Their Department of Fish Intelligence published a report on the relative IQ's of several game fish – including those commonly found in Oklahoma farm ponds. And sure enough, the carp, which I could never seem to catch, ranked in intelligence right up there with walleye and trout. The obvious conclusion, by some who know me, was that I am dumber than a carp. Others disagree based on the fact that the Flat Head Catfish, the dumbest of all fish tested, is also beyond my expertise.

Some medical reports state that eating fish might actually make one smarter. My conclusion from all of this is that if I eat lots of fish I might become smart enough to catch one.

Where Do They Go?

I have been wearing eyeglasses since I was twelve years old. Until about a decade ago one pair was all I needed. None were ever stolen or misplaced in all those years.

Then something began to happen. One day while I was shopping, someone stole my glasses right off of my face while I wasn't looking. I never saw them coming. And it had happened before. Restaurants are notorious for stealing glasses. One such place in Joplin had four pair of my glasses hidden in a drawer, and had the never to claim that I had left them there. It is as if a conspiracy has developed to keep me from reading menus and the prices of merchandise.

In self-defense I have begun to stockpile glasses. Spares are kept at my desk, at my computer, at my easy chair, in both cars, in my shop and on my tractor. There is also an extra pair, which I don't recognize, stored in my nightstand. However, if any more glasses go missing, it might be wise for me to start ordering them by the case.

What is with these people?

Gordon Thompson

My Court Martial

Occasionally my mind is filled with old memories of events that could have changed my life. One such event began in April 1944. That was the day our little ship, the FP-147, set out from San Pedro, California loaded with supplies for our troops on Guadalcanal. Our crew was mostly teen-agers like myself and a few seasoned seamen who had volunteered for this service. Our officers appeared to be capable and ready to perform our mission, especially our captain who looked like an admiral, complete with gold braid and uniform.

Our first indication of trouble came when we reached Honolulu. Two of the seasoned seamen jumped ship there claiming that the captain was crazy. Some of his actions had indeed seemed harsh and over-protective, but not unusual in a war zone I thought. The lost crewmembers were replaced and we proceeded on our way.

Our course to Guadalcanal would normally have taken us southwest to the Christmas Islands, then westward between the Marshall and Gilbert Island Groups, then through the Straits of Malaita to Guadalcanal. However, both groups of islands had been under Japanese control since Japan withdrew from the League of Nations in 1938, and air bases existed at Tarawa, in the Gilberts, and Kwajalein, in the Marshals. The gap between them was dangerous waters forcing us to detour to the south. Our captain decided to give a wide berth to any possible danger and took us hundreds of miles further south than was needed for safety.

Twenty-five days out of Honolulu we approached the Strait of Malaita, a narrow slit of water between Malaita and Santa Isabel Islands, in a mild tropical storm. Our navigator, who hadn't had a star fix in three days, advised the captain to slow down but we plowed on at full speed through the night. At midnight I was relieved at the ship's wheel, and proceeded forward to my cabin in the bow of the ship. Within minutes the ship struck a reef. There was bouncing and grinding as we swung broadside to the waves with the hull rolling several degrees to port. Believing perhaps that we were sinking the captain sounded "general quarters" to abandon ship. Both lifeboats were located near the stern. When we opened our door to the forward deck, heavy waves were flowing across, impeding our progress to the lifeboats. Unable to move we watched as both lifeboats were swung out for boarding. But before anyone could climb aboard both boats were smashed against the hull of the ship and fell into the sea with no one aboard.

The only remaining floatation devices large enough to save the crew were two large rafts, which were lashed to the rigging of the forward mast. The captain aimed his bullhorn in our direction and ordered us to launch the rafts. Normal launching procedure required climbing the rigging, cutting the bindings that secured the rafts to let them slide into the sea. Boarding would take place in the water. In teams of two we tied ourselves together to reduce risk of being washed overboard and headed for the rigging. Waves, now more than three feet deep, covered everything we would normally hold onto and made reaching the rigging unattainable. After several attempts we retreated to our cabin to await further orders.

Moments later the order came again to launch the rafts, even though no other crew members had been ordered to help us. Our second attempt ended in failure – like the first. In frustration we returned to our quarters wondering what to do next. The captain had witnessed our attempts and had offered no advice that might help us. We would wait until daybreak and try again.

By morning the waves had subsided somewhat and we could see that the ship had settled on the reef with only a foot of deck showing. We had taken water, which had actually held us in place and helped to keep us from sliding off the reef. The captain was waiting with his bullhorn. He aimed in our direction and informed us that we were under arrest and confined to quarters. Moments later the deck foreman (boatswain) approached carrying a container of food and wearing a side arm. He was grim and uncommunicative. He gave us the food and left quickly.

On the fourth day of our confinement a PBY Flying Boat

landed on the leeward side of the reef and removed all of the crew except the officers, the cook and us five seamen up front. The captain then summoned us to appear before him in his cabin. We stood at attention for several minutes before he spoke. I can remember almost word for word what he said:

"You men are being charged with mutiny in the second degree and with insubordination in time of war. You will be tried in a military court when we are freed from this rock. In the meantime, you will unload our cargo, all 2000 tons of it, so the ship can be repaired when rescue comes. Your work schedule will be six hours on and six hours off with thirty minutes for meals, no rest breaks and no talking between you. Your work will begin immediately. The boatswain will man the wenches and have control over you at all time. Obey what he says."

It was near one hundred degrees when we uncovered the hatches. The cargo was 40 lb. boxes of canned food with no handholds for grabbing and no cargo hooks were provided. It opened my eyes to what slavery really meant.

For nine days we worked without interruption until the rescue boats arrived. We were then locked back in our quarters so the workers could have access to the damaged hull. About two weeks later the hull was patched, the water pumped out and we were towed off the reef and southward to Espiritu Santo, New Hebrides for repairs. We were removed from the ship and placed in the Army Brig in individual cells.

Each of us was assigned a lawyer. My immediate concern was the maximum penalty I could get if convicted. Fortunately, we would be tried under civilian codes, which rules out the death penalty. The max was life in a federal prison with parole on good behavior.

We pleaded "Not Guilty" to all counts on council's recommendation and were briefed on how to give our testimony. We were treated well in our cells. My cell was never locked but, of course, there was no place to run.

Before I Forget

The trial dragged on through several hearings. The court moved from questioning me to getting my impression of the captain. I had to admit that I was afraid of the captain and would not voluntarily serve with him again. The court was courteous and attentive and seemed genuinely interested in doing the right thing.

The day finally came for a verdict. We were returned to the ship, now in dry-dock, and stood at attention as the court filled aboard. We saluted and they saluted back, but went directly to the captain's quarters upstairs. In a few minutes they came back down again and lined up directly in front of us, all nine of them, exactly like a firing squad, I thought.

We exchanged salutes again. Then the ranking officer stepped forward to read the verdict. I remember every word. "Boys," he said. "We find each of you 'Not Guilty'. You are free to go." As we filed off the deck they wished us well in our next assignment.

Our celebration was interrupted by the sight of our captain and first mate being taken off the ship in handcuffs. We never saw them again.

I served out my contract as crewman on a mortuary ship returning fallen soldiers to the National Graveyard at Hollandia, New Guinea.

Epilogue

Looking back over my lifetime, it is impossible to grasp the magnitude of God's Mercy and Grace that has protected and sustained me through the years.

Of the 215,000 Seamen who ran the ships during WWII, 8,300 went down with their ships. 12,000 others were wounded, of which 1,100 died from wounds inflicted by the enemy. And 663 were taken prisoner of war.

I suffered no physical injuries during the wars. However, Post Traumatic Stress Syndrome has prevented me from enjoying many of the pleasures of life, like washing dishes, cleaning house, and mowing lawns.

Unfortunately, my golf game was not affected by the war.

Merchant Seamen were granted Veteran Status by an act of congress in 1988, 43 years after the Peace Treaty was signed. But Seamen were not officially notified. I received my Official Discharge, granted by the United States Coast Guard, in June of 2010, 65 years after the war ended.

And I had almost forgotten.

References

The U.S. Weather Bureau

Various Internet References

BIOGRAPHICAL

Born: December 3, 1924

Marriage: To Elizabeth Margaret Mangini, May 3, 1953
    Daughters – Carol and Beth
    Grandchildren – Nicklas and Nathan

Military Service:

 World War II - Merchant Marines 1943-46
    Southwest Pacific war zone

Korean War - U.S. Army 2 years
    Heavy Antiaircraft Artillery

Education:
 Merchant Marine Seamanship School
 University of Oklahoma - BS Mechanical Engineering
 University of Tennessee – BS Science & Applied Arts

Work Experience:
 Research Engineer, E.I. DuPont 30 years
 Patents – eight

Religion:
 Southern Baptist:
 Deacon, 50 years
 Bible Teacher, 55 years
 Church Nuisance, most of the time

Travel:
 Most oceans and continents

Talents:
 Too few to mention

Things I'm Good At:
  Giving advice to anyone whom will listen (not many)

Future Plans:
  Getting up in the mornings; and, when I can't, going to Heaven.

Made in the USA
Columbia, SC
29 November 2022